" The Object Lessons series achieves something close to magic: the books take ordinary—even banal—objects and animate them with a rich history of invention, political struggle, science, and popular mythology. Filled with fascinating details and conveyed in sharp, accessible prose, the books make the everyday world come to life. Be warned: once you've read a few of these, you'll start walking around your house, picking up random objects, and musing aloud: 'I wonder what the story is behind this thing?'"

Steven Johnson, author of *Where Good Ideas Come From* and *How We Got to Now*

" In 1957 the French critic and semiotician Roland Barthes published *Mythologies*, a groundbreaking series of essays in which he analysed the popular culture of his day, from laundry detergent to the face of Greta Garbo, professional wrestling to the Citroën DS. This series of short books, Object Lessons, continues the tradition."

Melissa Harrison, *Financial Times*

" Though short, at roughly 25,000 words apiece, these books are anything but slight."

Marina Benjamin, *New Statesman*

The joy of the series, of reading *Remote Control*, *Golf Ball*, *Driver's License*, *Drone*, *Silence*, *Glass*, *Refrigerator*, *Hotel*, and *Waste* (more titles are listed as forthcoming) in quick succession, lies in encountering the various turns through which each of their authors has been put by his or her object. As for Benjamin, so for the authors of the series, the object predominates, sits squarely center stage, directs the action. The object decides the genre, the chronology, and the limits of the study. Accordingly, the author has to take her cue from the *thing* she chose or that chose her. The result is a wonderfully uneven series of books, each one a *thing* unto itself."

Julian Yates, *Los Angeles Review of Books*

The Object Lessons project, edited by game theory legend Ian Bogost and cultural studies academic Christopher Schaberg, commissions short essays and small, beautiful books about everyday objects from shipping containers to toast. *The Atlantic* hosts a collection of 'mini object-lessons'. . . . More substantive is Bloomsbury's collection of small, gorgeously designed books that delve into their subjects in much more depth."

Cory Doctorow, *Boing Boing*

. . . a sensibility somewhere between Roland Barthes and Wes Anderson."

Simon Reynolds, **author of** *Retromania: Pop Culture's Addiction to Its Own Past*

OBJECTLESSONS

A book series about the hidden lives of ordinary things.

Series Editors:

Ian Bogost and Christopher Schaberg

Advisory Board:

Sara Ahmed, Jane Bennett, Jeffrey Jerome Cohen,
Johanna Drucker, Raiford Guins, Graham Harman,
renée hoogland, Pam Houston, Eileen Joy, Douglas
Kahn, Daniel Miller, Esther Milne, Timothy Morton,
Kathleen Stewart, Nigel Thrift, Rob Walker, Michele White.

In association with

LOYOLA UNIVERSITY NEW ORLEANS   Georgia Tech | Center for Media Studies

BOOKS IN THE SERIES

tree

MATTHEW BATTLES

with photographs by
Sarah W. Newman

Bloomsbury Academic
An imprint of Bloomsbury Publishing Inc

B L O O M S B U R Y
NEW YORK · LONDON · OXFORD · NEW DELHI · SYDNEY

Bloomsbury Academic

An imprint of Bloomsbury Publishing Inc

1385 Broadway
New York
NY 10018
USA

50 Bedford Square
London
WC1B 3DP
UK

www.bloomsbury.com

**BLOOMSBURY and the Diana logo are trademarks of
Bloomsbury Publishing Plc**

First published 2017

Library of Congress Cataloging-in-Publication Data
A catalog record for this book is available from the Library of Congress.

ISBN: PB: 978-1-6289-2051-2
ePub: 978-1-6289-2053-6
ePDF: 978-1-6289-2054-3

Series: Object Lessons

Cover design: Alice Marwick
Photographs © Sarah W. Newman

Typeset by Deanta Global Publishing Services, Chennai, India
Printed and bound in the United States of America

CONTENTS

PART THREE   A DARK ABUNDANCE

PART ONE

FERAL TREES

The tree of heaven

Can a tree be feral?

It's a question I've been asking ever since I started frequenting Bussey Brook Meadow, a twenty-four-acre pennant of land pinned between a sunken railroad right-of-way and a swooping city road. The meadow is part of the Arnold Arboretum—a nearly three-hundred-acre collection of trees and shrubs and the largest jewel in the "Emerald Necklace," the chain of parkways that adorns Boston, binding Back Bay and the downtown to hilly neighborhoods in Dorchester, Roxbury, and Jamaica Plain. The collection of the Arboretum consists of more than ten thousand trees, shrubs, and vines. Each one of these plants has a number, emblazoned on a metallic tag, which indicates its place in a database. For each tree, a geographic origin is noted, as well as a genealogy in seed, rootstock, or graft; every intervention, every pruned limb or aeration of roots, is documented and archived as well. In the Arboretum, the trees are *domesticated*—or at the very least, they're *tame*. Later, I'll discuss these terms—wild and domesticated, tame and feral—to see if we can use them to think about some of the salient-but-hidden qualities not only of trees and other creatures, but possibly objects of all kinds. In the Arboretum, it's safe to say, a clement domesticity rules: trees clad the puddingstone hills that evoke Boston's primordial topography; trees make shadow-heavy frames for greenswards and mazy plantings of lilac and rose; trees enfold bubbling brooks tasted by lapping dogs and soft tongues of sunlight.

In Bussey Brook Meadow, just across the park road dappled by the overspreading hemlocks and sycamores, conditions (environmental and curatorial) are starkly different from those that obtain in the Arboretum proper. At the long, south-stabbing point of the meadow, a marsh rises, given over to a troika of wetland plants: yellow-flag iris; native cattail; and the well-traveled, cosmopolitan reed *Phragmites*, its tall green spears thrusting in oblique profusion, each sharpened tip brusquely decorated with a dun lace of flower. To the north, the plot tilts and rises, the ground thrust up by many decades of construction waste and sheer rubbish piled up by successive waves of building in the surrounding neighborhood. A melange of tree species, many of them seed-escapees from the Arboretum—cottonwood, red maple, catalpa—have taken firm hold of the bank that rises from the water table.

Although Bussey Brook Meadow is managed by the Arboretum, the trees there have no tags. They are not accessioned, tracked, or described in any database. The Arboretum administers the meadow (strange formula, *to administer a meadow*) as an "urban wild," a stretch of open land left to do what open land does in the city: to weave a skein of native and invasive plant species especially tolerant of salt, heat, and heavy metals; to reprise Darwin's tangled bank in a metropolitan key. Where the hillside steepens, a tangled vinescape of grape and oriental bittersweet is shaken here and there by the passage of a rat or the metabolic hijinks of songbirds. And towering up out of this tangle, a ragged line of trees—tall with thin, toppling trunks, sinuous and smooth, glowing palely in the shade of their own latticed, breeze-lively canopy—stand like a war party advancing on the ruderal meadow, making forest from the bruised and dented land. At their feet, a shag of saplings carpets the edge of the path, densely interwoven foliage which, when torn, exudes a nutty, musky aroma.

With its rank odor in my nostrils, I ask again: can a tree—can *these* trees, specifically—be feral?

The species of tree prompting the question—of which that row of slender, tall specimens are splendid examples—was named *Ailanthus altissima* by Linnaeus, and is now commonly known as the Tree of Heaven. To call it a species, of course, is already to engage in a peculiar way of doing and thinking with trees and other objects. Trees after all manifest as species, but as many other kinds and collocations of things as well.

It is midsummer as I write, and everywhere the *Ailanthus* are in full fruit, boughs heavy with great clusters of key-like samaras—the twisty-winged seeds by which *Ailanthus* makes itself prolific—in tones of rose-red and green-gold. Their trunks are sinuous, gracile, with gray speckled bark that seems to luminesce in shade and all but disappears in sunlight; the broad, compound leaves, palmate and many-membered, sway readily in the breeze. Once you recognize its foliage, you begin to see *Ailanthus* everywhere, in precarious neighborhoods, along highways, and in the shabby, ruderal edgelands especially. By habit and quality, *Ailanthus* seeks out and colonizes the margins, where modern concepts of property find their slippery limits: at the edges of public rights of way; in the upthrust jointures of the concrete slabs making an uneasy alley between apartment buildings; along the bent and ragged sheets of chain-link fence that quarter the empty lots. For *Ailanthus*, to a degree unmatched by any other tree in North America native or invasive, is feral and ungovernable. It is the tree that will not be owned.

Later I'll explain what I mean by this word, *feral*, and what I find useful in it for conjecturing certain kinds of relations not only among trees and other living things, but objects of many kinds. But it's important for me to assert, this early in the argument, that it is the trees—uncanny, possessed of depths and mystery, and feral in ways beyond my ken— which take priority over any terminology.

In my swooning pursuit of feral trees, I've had friends and collaborators. The first of these was Kyle Parry, who was a Harvard graduate student in film and visual studies when we joined forces. At the time, we were exploring the possibility of developing a kind of mobile curatorial application for the Arboretum (a possibility which never took shape, although many good things came of our connection with the Arboretum and its staff); Kyle, with his generous intelligence and reflective curiosity, had taken up the task of managing the collaboration. His finely fibered imagination found much to dilate upon in the Arboretum, with its living collection and its ramifying, baroque, even mannered evocation of wildness in the city. And together, we were both captured by the spell of Bussey Brook Meadow—and *Ailanthus* in particular.

The spell was that of the Tree of Heaven, but the magician who cast it was Peter Del Tredici, botanist and senior researcher at the Arboretum (now retired) and a lecturer at Harvard's Graduate School of Design, who has made a special project of Bussey Brook Meadow. One seething, mosquito-droning summer day, Kyle and I met up with Peter along the meadow's gravel path, where he had proposed to orient us to the site and its feral riches. Del Tredici, at once avuncular and acerbic, has a way of hooding his eyes and veiling his countenance as he creeps up on a conjecture about trees or the people who care about them. Speaking, he casts out his vowels like bait on a long line—and we rose to it eagerly, time and again.

Peter spoke not of weeds nor even invasives, but of "cosmopolitan communities" of "spontaneous vegetation"; peering with him into the tangled bank of *Ailanthus* festooned with bittersweet, porcelain berry, mugwort, cocklebur, and Virginia creeper, we saw a nature not ruled by laws, but relationships, qualities, expression, *affect*. Plants tell stories through their habits of growth, their manner of flourishing and dying back, their blossoming and seed-dispersal (forms of vegetal activity termed *phenology* by botanists). And these cosmopolitan species, with ways and natures deeply imbricated in human worlds, tell stories of feral forms of urban biology that transcend bare life to form a *bios* rich, unruly, and overspilling with dark abundance, a productively unstinting mystery.

Waving his arms demonstratively before a stand of staghorn sumac or a tapestry of wild grapevine, Peter would catalog the "ecosystem services" of such natural-cultural fellow travelers—their bioremediation of heavy metals, their softening of sunlight and tempering of fierce urban microclimates, their treasuring-up of carbon. But we understood that it was the spirit of these hardy, flourishing fellow travelers that mattered to him most. Del Tredici is the author of the deceptively anodyne *Wild Urban Plants of the Northeast: A Field Guide,*[1] which identifies and describes several hundred of the plant species (including *Ailanthus*) most frequently seen engulfing fences, lining alleyways, and sprouting from sidewalk cracks. His book transforms the green haze at the edge of urban scenes into a vital, diverse riot of expressive creatures, an effect which can be deeply and richly disruptive to one's daily commute.

I'm not sure how *Ailanthus* came to serve as the objective correlative of this engagement for Kyle and me, but we fell hard—and fast. Our zeal was spurred, surely, as we looked around on our walk back to the subway after leaving Peter in the meadow—at the edge of which, along the jumbled and clumsy stone walls, *Ailanthus* sprouted in clumps and quantities; and here it was again, a trio of seedlings, likely suckering clones and thus a budding superorganism, jutting up from the cracked concrete of the traffic island; and there again, its chandelier boughs swaying vigorously far above the commuter railway as the train whisked us back into the city. The tree spoke up, and we found ourselves looking for every chance to listen.

But we wandered, in our scholarly wont, as much among books and arguments, archives and image sets, as forest paths and abandoned back lots, for a point of purchase on this unruly other. It was Kyle who found an evocative quote from the experimental filmmaker Trinh Minh-ha, with her gentle advice to "speak nearby," that came to serve as our charter: to offer "a speaking that does not objectify, does not point to an object as if it is distant from the speaking subject or absent from the speaking place"—

A speaking that reflects on itself and can come very close to a subject without, however, seizing or claiming it. A speaking in brief, whose closures are only moments of transition opening up to other possible moments of transition—these are forms of indirectness well understood by anyone in tune with poetic language. . . . Because actually, this is not just a technique or a statement to be made verbally. It is an attitude in life, a way of positioning oneself in relation to the world. . . . Truth never yields itself in anything said or shown. One cannot just point a camera at it to catch it: the very effort to do so will kill it. . . . Truth can only be approached indirectly if one does not want to lose it and find oneself hanging on to a dead, empty skin. Even when the indirect has to take refuge in the very figures of the direct, it continues to defy the closure of a direct reading. (Chen 1992)[2]

As we sidled up alongside *Ailanthus*, then, we did so not only in its worldly habitats, but in its haunts in cultural history as well. A feral approach to feral creatures.

And in its pursuit, we discovered, we had taken up with a disreputable character. In the library, but also in dialogue with gardeners, arborists, and others who count themselves knowledgeable with respect to trees, shrubs, and all green-growing things woody and herbaceous, *Ailanthus* is a scourge. To utter its name in the presence of arborists or gardeners is to elicit groans and puffs of acrimony and indignation. *Ailanthus altissima* has been stamped with the black mark of classical ecology: it is denominated a "noxious invasive." Its habitual profusion strikes fear into the lover of ordered landscape; its musky odor reveals a rankness that works in the botanical world as wantonly as in the animal; with its clonal, suckering habit, it is nearly impossible to cut back or eradicate—cut short a sapling at ground level and three more spring up, clones from the same rootstock. And finally, it is a native of China—a lineage, which, although shared with many splendid and well-loved ornamental trees, including *Metasequoia* and the ubiquitous Gingko, did *Ailanthus* little credit in the ugly yellow-peril climate of the nineteenth century when it first proliferated in American cities. The Asian origin of *Ailanthus* haunts it still, as Americans toil with an ill-formed knot of fear and resentment of China and all it can seem to represent in a shifting, uncertainly ordered world.

But *Ailanthus* takes up this suspect character, this feral reputation, over a lengthy cultural history. It is the eponymous tree of Betty Smith's novel, *A Tree Grows in Brooklyn*, where it marks the passage of a neighborhood from native civility to the unruly decline of immigration:

> You took a walk on a Sunday afternoon and came to a nice neighborhood, very refined. You saw a small one of these trees through the iron gate leading to someone's yard and you knew that soon that section of Brooklyn would be a tenement district. The tree knew. It came there first. Afterwards, poor foreigners seeped in and the quiet old brownstone houses were hacked up into flats, feather beds were pushed out onto window sills to air and the Tree of Heaven flourished.[3]

When the tree first made its appearance in the West, many of the qualities that lend its invasive habits energy and strength were not feared but prized. In the eighteenth century, *Ailanthus* was among the exotics growing in the Philadelphia garden of John Bartram, colonial America's preeminent botanist. In the early nineteenth century, the tree was appraised in cool and anodyne terms, and the disputes it occasioned were restricted to botanical discourse; by the end of the nineteenth century, however, *Ailanthus* had become a slippery character, at once an avatar of leafy vitality and a harbinger of civilization's eventual fall. "The plant spreads vigorously by offshoots as well as by seed, and it has been said of it, that if, by some dire calamity, New York should fall in ruin and for a time be uninhabited, it would in a few years be covered with a forest of *Ailanthus*."[4]

The city fallen, post apocalyptic, a ruin of *Ailanthus*: an image from the turn of the last century with resonance in our own, collapse-haunted era. The connection wasn't lost on Kyle and me—in our unofficial, wandering census, we were seeing the Tree of Heaven everywhere: laughing in the wind-tunnel gale of the Massachusetts Turnpike, festooning the overpasses and dusty, gravel-flecked lots of Somerville's Sullivan Square, or sprouting with hungry insistence from between close-set triple-deckers in urban neighborhoods. In its native forest setting, *Ailanthus* acts as a "gap obligate," spotting holes in the canopy and growing with slender urgency to take advantage of them; thus it readily flourishes in narrow alleys and breezeways, liminal spaces of uncertain propriety. If an *Ailanthus* ecology is the future of the twenty-first-century city, we realized, it is already here, however unevenly distributed.

Kyle and I were soon joined in this hunt for feral trees by Sarah Newman, an artist and photographer who came to our lab as a fellow in the fall of 2013. Sarah brought a ready commitment to the "forms of indirectness" described by Trinh Minh-ha, a habit of making visible some of the hidden qualities of immanent things. It was she who led us to attend especially to the humans who live in proximity with *Ailanthus*—provoking us to stand, without seizing or claiming, closer to them.

Like Kyle and me, Sarah quickly came to spot *Ailanthus* wherever it sprouted—from the shadowed narrows of an alley; through the chain-link of a high-voltage transformer installation; in profusion as a thicket of seedlings in an untended front yard. Prowling Somerville on long solo shooting expeditions, Sarah found a flourishing stand of *Ailanthus* edging a Union Square parking lot, where an elderly couple of Southeast Asian descent staged their can-and-bottle operation. They parked their shopping carts and bulging bags of returnables in the vaulted shade of Trees of Heaven towering together in the corner of the lot. The woman, in a version of traditional dress that seemed pieced together from thrift-store finds, demurely stood before the chain-link fence, talking *sotto voce* in her lovely, barbed language, while Sarah shot her portrait, the man meanwhile smilingly busying himself with the couple's treasury of aluminum and glass. Behind them, the chain-link copse of *Ailanthus*, going golden already with the approach of autumn, dodged and bounded in the sun. Elsewhere, near the Cambridge Public Library, Sarah caught a moment with a teenage girl, elegantly shy in a simple flowing dress and headphones, standing beneath a tall *Ailanthus* leaning out of a primly fenced backyard. And then there was the remarkable Symphor—wheelchair-bound, spry of eye and quick of humor—who in thirty years living in the same apartment had watched the dooryard *Ailanthus* go from a sapling to a solid tree gracefully overtopping his triple-decker building. From Ivory Coast, Symphor had come to Cambridge to study math at MIT, his wheels taking who knows how many turns while the *Ailanthus* patiently poured itself into emanation by the front stoop.

We were making images, gathering words, saying our greetings to the feral trees at every subway station and back alley. As fall gave way to winter's winds, the *Ailanthus* offered up their seeds, which spun away in unruly flocks; gales stripped the golden leaflets and flung them about like banknotes, leaving petioles bare, bereft. The lush carpets of seedlings in the vacant lots disappeared entirely beneath drifts of snow. In the midst of a blizzard one night in a vacant lot in Union Square, flashing lights transfixed the pelting snow, catching the trees of the parking lot in their patience, their attention, their raw and speckled winter nudity. I imagined a murmur of discourse stirring in the dormant roots, a flicker of sugar and phenols rattling up from the frozen fill beneath the snow-secreted asphalt:

Snow plunders the city. There is a bag in the branches. In a limb-patrolled precinct, the snow's prison is battered into shape by wind and by injured fences.

Already fingering the locks of summer's golden hair, sap grasps earth along all these channels. Make a body of the fences, a body embracing the broken asphalt, radical and full, sustaining the sleepers below.

Rumored in the shudder of the bus, we keep our treasury of snow. We're given of winter, sun gone underground, netted in the roots, shards of it buried in the sapwood.

Flashing lights churn the streets, there is a clot and rumble, a cavitation of sleepless machines that stumble and avalanche away.

Rooted in the speckled wind. Counting, shuddering, weighing the burden of the sky. We're together, the others are here too. And in this treasury of snow, broken houses, and the bags of history, the seeds of appetite abide. Falling ice catches shards of remembered light, shatters in the flash, turns to spray in the vines' dark weave. And the trees of winter count their riches.

In a dappled world

The approach I take in this book to *Ailanthus*—the approach I broadly take to the tree as an object—will be dappled. I'm inspired to take this approach not only by the patterns of light and shade trees make, but also by the work of philosopher of science Nancy Cartwright, who argues that, taken together, scientific "laws" can never assemble a coherent and unified picture of the world. Instead, our theorems—Newton's Third Law; natural selection; the concept of the climax community in classical ecology—describe phenomena that are framed by the controlled conditions of the laboratory or the special descriptive tools of fieldwork. The light these ideas shed on actual things and events is always oblique, refractory, and surrounded by depths of shadows. As Cartwright puts it, "We live in a dappled world"—

> a world rich in different things, with different natures, behaving in different ways. The laws that describe this world are a patchwork, not a pyramid. They do not take after the simple, elegant and abstract structure of a system of axioms and theorems. Rather they look like . . . erratic overlaps; here and there, once in a while, corners that line up, but mostly ragged edges; and always the cover of law just loosely attached to the jumbled world of material things.[1]

The dappled light of *Tree* filters through the variety of knowledge practices that discipline and constrain our attention to the natural world: ecology, evolutionary biology, and horticulture, as well as philology, natural history, and landscape studies. These knowledge practices are all useful; they all shed light. But they are insufficient.

In the modern era, *Ailanthus*, like all living things, falls under the rule of ecology, a discipline that comes with a strict and normative morality (which after all is only in the nature of a discipline). Ecology's outlook is prelapsarian: in its classic view, life naturally tends toward the grandeur of continuity and tempered, well-wrought balance. Intact ecosystems are those unsullied by human presence, impelled naturally in unstinting progress toward a state of climax, a collective, stately condition of maturity and unassailable stasis. The essential formulation of this perspective was given by Aldo Leopold, who in his book *A Sand County Almanac* articulates what he called "the land ethic": "A thing is right when it tends to preserve the integrity, stability, and beauty of the biotic community," Leopold writes. "It is wrong when it tends otherwise."[2]

Introduced into such peaceable kingdoms, the invasive species is one capable of disturbing this well-wrought equilibrium; lacking local enemies, unfamiliar to the evolutionarily refined tastes of browsing herbivores or hungry meat-eaters, the invasive species is the specter of collapse that haunts the ordered certainties of classical ecology. Invasive plant species exhibit unruly habits: in their promiscuity, they produce vast quantities of offspring; they readily colonize disturbed, compacted, or polluted soils; they contend readily with rocky aridity and chemical cascades. When exhibited in wild margins—say, the barrens of newly upthrust volcanic islands—such qualities make plants into pioneers, and ecology loves the tales of abundance and renewal such species tell in situations of naturally occurring precarity unsullied by the anthropic. Ecology tells stories about the succession and climax of biota, stories that recapitulate human progress in a wild key: the tropical island begins as a sulfurous basalt carbuncle rising steaming from the waves, cooling to black and sterile rock; seeds blown by the trade winds lodge in cracks, putting down roots that break down the basalt and treasure up soil. Species that affect this transformation share a complex of features: hardiness, high dispersal capacity, ability to subsist on meager resources. In time more colonists arrive on the winds and waves (coconut palms; insects lodged in the feathers of migratory birds), until a flourishing community of plants and animals achieves its climax state in the form of a tropical forest. The crucial phase in such succession stories, for our purposes, is the first one, the point at which the first hardy seeds arrive on disturbed ground and begin a process of biologization: in a context framed as "natural," these species are understood to perform crucial tasks that prepare the terrain for occupation— turning a dead landscape into a biome. Such communities are referred to in classical ecology as "pioneer flora."[3] Like the city, the volcanic island is characterized by "high levels of disturbance, impervious paving, and heat retention";[4] thus it should not surprise us that it is the qualities of disturbance-tolerant, so-called early successional "pioneer flora" which, in the urban environment, make a plant a weed. The same qualities that can make a species a pioneer in one context, mark it as invasive in places where the prelapsarian paradigm of nativity and ordered progress reigns: in wild lands, in parks and preserves, and even in our cities.

And yet the denomination "weed" is not merely an arbitrary pejorative. It sticks to species sharing a set of habits and characteristics that tie them to human forms of life. The British botanist E. J. Salisbury, who pursued the ecological study of weeds, describes this complex symbiosis in the context of deep human history: as "many species of weeds may have evolved during the morainic conditions of the long glacial period," he points out, "it is not without significance that this was contemporaneous with the later environmental changes that man has brought about upon the earth's surface."[5] This move is interesting: against the standard botanical polemic that the word "weed" has no biological meaning, Salisbury argues, "weediness" is a biotic habit, a way in the world, for plants manifesting a symbiosis with this peculiarly convivial, wandering, tool-bearing species, *Homo sapiens*.

Companioned to the insistent weeds, Salisbury says, there exists a shadow biome of fellow travelers whose lives have been bound up with our species' fortunes in hidden ways. "The cosmopolitan occurrence of many weeds," Salisbury writes, "bears two characteristics: their remarkable plasticity and tolerance of a wide range of environmental conditions, and the efficiency of their dispersal, perhaps often by human agency. . . . It is a salutary thought, which students of geographical distribution may be reluctant to concede, that the same efficiency of dispersal may well have characterized also species that are far less tolerant of disturbed conditions . . . and which therefore do not, by their occurrence, betray the probability that they may owe their wide distribution to human agency."[6] Even prior to the Neolithic Revolution, the migration of humans worldwide may have spurred a weedy dispersal of pioneer species following in train. "Many of the weeds of cultivated and waste ground have become so widely distributed over the surface of the globe that . . . their region of origin is often extremely problematical."[7]

Exploring the cultural roles dogs play in human life, the critic and philosopher of science Donna Haraway has described the canine as a "companion species": "partners in the crime of human evolution," Haraway writes, "[dogs] are in the garden from the get-go, wily as Coyote."[8] Extending Haraway's pursuit of such "companion species," we might claim for the weeds a certain neighborliness. Our fellow travelers, they are the characteristic flora of the Anthropocene, companion species by one or two degrees of separation. And in this, we find an ally in Aldo Leopold, who wrote that his intention in formulating the land ethic was to enlarge "the boundaries of the community to include soils, waters, plants, and animals, or collectively . . ." to change "the role of *Homo sapiens* from conqueror of the land-community to plain member and citizen of it."[9] Clearly, this community could be extended to include our friends and companions, the weeds.

A branching heuristic

The worlds we make for living things to inhabit, invade, and contest often resolve as polarities: the wild and the pastoral; the thickly settled and the ruderal; emergent and the climactic; urban and agricultural. Within their dichotomous dance, these worlds infiltrate and interpenetrate one another in dappled and contrary ambiguity—and it's in their midst that I want to explore this question of the feral more fully. Now that *Ailanthus* is a familiar neighbor species, the question of arborescent ferality arises frequently: as I fly down I-95 in light morning traffic, walk to the train station in my Boston neighborhood, or stand in the midst of a parking lot in Somerville. It arises for me most often when I am in transit, for the trees that prompt the question are themselves creatures of transit—and, though movement is imperceptible to us except in traces, they are creatures *in* transit as well.

These qualities of transience, liberty, and ungovernability readily associate with ferality, and gather as a set of terms with strong family resemblances. But I want to say that by "feral" I mean something quite specific: a condition, flickering and manifold, with its own dark abundance of qualities, which helps to crack open or expand the troublesome paradigm of wildness and domestication. Where humankind dichotomizes, the world problematizes. A response I find useful is to put a binary such as *wild/domesticated* through a series of semiotic twists and turns, to break it or expand it into a field.[1]

Wild ⟷ *Domesticated*

A train flows through the neighborhood now, breezing down the long vector of the canalized right-of-way, ratcheting along the many-miled, open-mouthed grin of the concrete ties, the smirched and cindered ridgeway of roadbed gravel; at its air-tearing passage, the leaves of Ailanthus *rattle and sway, rebound, caress, describe narrowing cones of green-infused shadow.*

Let us parse what the terms *wild* and *domesticated* might usefully be said to mean. Wild and domestic: the terms have long danced in English. *Wilde* appears in the ninth-century *Corpus Glossary*, where it glosses the Latin word *indomitus*—a word associated by more than phonetic similarity with the domestic. The wild is that which is not dominated, not governed, also that which does not take shelter in a house. For the ninth-century English imagination, organizing the world according to that which resides inside or outside, is walled in or beyond the pale, exists *in horto* or excommunicate, was an impulse more than convenient. In the early Middle Ages, the garden walls already are thick, and old, and in need of constant maintenance. By training and by breeding—by what Darwin called "artificial selection," although it is as natural a process as anywhere humans are concerned—the domesticated creature is brought into the human *domus*, domiciled with us and within us.

In terms of natural history, the domesticated creature has made a bargain, tying itself to our own species' restless sociality and habitual flexibility. Domesticated creatures share certain characteristics: they lose their astringency, their sharpness of tooth or thorn, much of their wariness. Such characteristics dropped for efficiency as much as human convenience; defensiveness is expensive, and the domesticated do well to place the burden on us humans. In return they gain fats, sugars, intensities of affect in flash of eye and beauty of bloom. Domestication is profoundly a strange case of symbiosis—one with echoes and ramifications in cultural realms beyond the ken of biology. We're in pastoral territory here, in the high, dappled fields where flocks range, where vines trail and grow heavy with grape—and indeed, domestication is much older than civilization, an artifact of the dreamtime communities of plants, animals, and human society described in mythology. And as in myth, it's hard to tell who is the top dog, the master gardener: the humans or the domesticated creatures, who proliferate by dint of this bargain with *Homo sapiens*.

Despite their opposition, both wild and domesticated creatures are at home in their worlds. To the sheep or the almond tree, pasture and orchard are worlds in full, in a profound sense complementary to the "natural habitat" that is the *habitus* of the wild. We might say that together they comprise the dimension of the *heimlich*, that which is at home in the world—"homely" beings, cozy and familiar, who typify qualities opposed to the uncanny (*unheimlich*, as Freud formulated the term).[2]

Complex and cosmological, there's no place like home.

Where the marked path bends toward the station, an improbable grove of Ailanthus *towers out of the sumac and grapevine, a filtry wall of thin-branching trunks, gray-glowing and serpentine, rocking in wind-sprung animation. They fix the crumble of the slope, rob light from the cottonwoods on the hilltop, push back the grape and bittersweet vinescape that tries to grip the lower hillside and steal its way to the sun. This war plays out in the seeming stillness of diurnal flexion and relaxation, in concentration of sugars and infinitesimal crescendos of cavitation, measured by the rhythm of sunrise and sunset that is a flicker in the land's long gaze.*

There are many ways to *do* wild and domesticated. Even with respect to the arboreal, there are many settled schools and practices for addressing trees and invoking their qualities: the forester's ways, and the lumberjack's; the nature lover's; the natural historian's; the arborist's or horticulturalist's; the paleontologist's. Perhaps we could go so far as to say that all the ways we know to think trees, to *do* trees, serve to chart the homely regions, the domicile of the cosmos. All of the ways in which it's *not* practical and normative to relate to trees— the interpersonal; the oneiric and mystical; the divine and animistic; the magical, and many ways and wisdoms simply as yet unrevealed—fall into the neuter territory, the region of the *not*. With that which is wild, there must also be the *not-wild*; likewise with the domesticated, there must also be a category, glimmering and vast, which could be described as *not-domesticated*. Both are zones of purely possible qualities, immanent and imaginal, beyond the pale and outside our experience. This is the dimension of the other, the *Unheimlich*—the uncanny—a veiled land of mystery and excess. Perhaps in the not-wild we have things of bare life, of *zoë*, which present themselves inert and yet uncannily fully formed: stones, storms, pinecones, pieces of things. Perhaps the fallen trees of the forest, soundless and undiscovered, reside here? In the not-domestic, meanwhile, we have the excesses of the abode: food, waiting to be consumed or lying in crumbs and smudges after a meal; the dying embers in the hearth, glowing with the waning animation of their own secret thoughts; the pure, polluting appearance of dirt (Mary Douglas's "matter out of place"[3]), arriving unannounced; sprouted potatoes in the pantry, bloom of mold on cheese, wintry drift of mothwings in the closet—unruly elements of the household that signify its ephemerality, portend its dissolution.

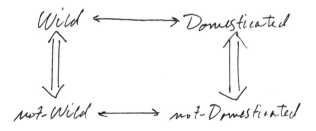

Sprung and unbuttressed, the long chandelier-curving limbs of Ailanthus *reach out over chain-link to overspread the highway. Where traffic rolls, rubber-rimmed and reckless, the boughs dance and feed the wind, their red-glowing cluster of seeds scintillate, treasured.*

In each of these dimensions, the homely and the uncanny, hybridities may be mapped. In the homely realm, the hybrid caught between *wild* and *domestic* is the tame creature, which has been disciplined, trained, bent to will, turned into a thing. There is a crucial temporal and individual aspect to this: tameness is not a thing that persists from generation to generation. If a tame creature bears offspring, those offspring, too, must be tamed if continuity is to be maintained. To tame takes tools, gear, equipment, *weapons*: leash and harness, muzzle and whip; as well as food and succor. This is because the qualities of tameness are imposed by force—its constant threat, its capricious relief. The lion in the cage, the orca in the pool, the oak pruned for the passage of electrical wires—these are tamed creatures, bent and broken, yoked and grafted. Thus tame is the hybrid caught, pacing and uneasy, between the wild and the domesticated.

And finally, in the hybrid zone of the neutral field, we find our ferality. Suspended between the *not-wild* and the *not-domesticated*, the *feral* creature is liminal: not so much caught betwixt and between as the vital avatar of betweenness itself. Hermes, messenger and shape-shifter, is the ancient avatar of the feral. Ferality, to paraphrase the cultural critic George

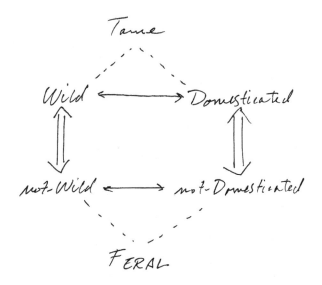

Trow, is the quality of having no qualities.[4] The feral creature: a domesticated animal forced by circumstance to adopt the wild estate; a beast caught in the betwixt and between; a traveler, and perhaps a kind of messenger as well. Its predicament is a familiar one; who has not felt it—stalking through an airport on the edge of lost, bruised and tickled by the terminal's uncanny familiarity; standing in line, waiting for a cup of coffee or a job; parked before the screen, hunching and bowing before social media's throbbing inquisition— who has not felt the prickle, the vague disquiet, of quarry? The domesticated creature has its limited phrasebook of human exchange, but in exile, beyond the habits of home, the glossary is splintered and uncertain. Like weeds—and the "weed" is the very feral expression of botanical being—we grow in disturbed soil, courting progress and collapse. Feral creatures subsist like the last speakers of a lost tongue; they utter their secrets without fear or hope of discovery.

It's important to remember that this diagramming of mine reveals no law of the universe. I'm drawing here from William James, who argues that "*nature is but a name for excess*":

> Every point in her opens out and runs into the more; and the only question, with reference to any point we may be considering, is how far into the rest of nature we may have to go in order to get entirely beyond its overflow. In the pulse of inner life immediately present now in each of us is a little past, a little future, a little awareness of our own body, of each other's persons, of these sublimities we are trying to talk about, of the earth's geography and the direction of history, of truth and error, of good and bad, and of who knows how much more?[5]

It's one of our supreme fictions that the landscapes, the elemental forces, the creatures of the world, all align in relation to *us*. Some of the subtler styles for such ordering—some of the pictures we offer the world and ask it to color, to animate—concern the stories we tell about wildness and domestication. These are slippery concepts, to be sure, which name only partially and provisionally assemblages of qualities and forces that elude discipline, comprehensiveness and quintessence. These concepts are nowhere stable and certain; across cultures and historicities they rhyme and chime in uncertain timbres. They are nowhere *a priori* or absolute; they have no fixed definition, but manifest a range of family resemblances. From a certain vantage point, a certain set of coordinates in human time and space, these concepts, the *domesticated* and the *wild*, emerge, take on salience and force. Behind or beyond these concepts, hosts and flocks of qualities withdraw from consideration, retreat into the glimmering immanence and indwelling mystery of objects, the dark abundance of the neutral field.

The world of William James—this nature of excess— prefigures the philosopher of science Nancy Cartwright's account of the world as a dappled place: forces and effects stream through it, clotted and variable, impelled less by law (universal, discrete, and discernible) than poetry. The world is the realm of mimicry and seduction—of the resonance and complement and play of art—of structures that emerge and cohere, bubbling and ephemeral, merging and rupturing into one another. My charting of wild and domestic, tame and feral, is no grammar or paradigm but a sketch, a mapping, a choreography. Perhaps it's an erotics, shadowing forth the tumble of affinity and disruption.

Rude fence of vagrant granite, its blocks refugees from far-off forces of upthrust and seismic pressure; along its craggy hip, an unmowed verge of turf where seedlings of Ailanthus *crowd and thrust. They are the jumbled memories of the tall tree in the distance, its own sapling forgotten, pale sliver of vegetal self deep in its heartwood, a ligneous flame still flickering from the secret red seed laid so long ago.*

The work that wildness does: there are wild men, wild beasts, wild places; in this ravening matrix, the possibility of trees wild and feral might seem barren, forced. Trees may seem more readily to manifest their wildness in quantity, as forest or wood, as the German *Wald*, which as we've encountered it shares some originary force with wildness as a word. But taken as an object, can something like a tree—sessile, fructifying, clement—*be* wild? This is where trees take up the qualities of static objects that yet uncannily move, grow, lift, shelter, injure, bleed, breed, flourish, senesce, and die. Trees can do work not only as wild, but as wilding as well.

In the last couple of decades, the concept of *rewilding* has gained popularity: the notion that through a series of management interventions, humans might restore stable ecosystems where they believe them to have fallen into ruins. Serious initiatives have been proposed to renew the buffalo-strewn Great Plains of North America or Europe's "Mammoth Steppe"; in well-funded labs, biologists seek the unwieldy assemblage of sequenced genes, modern candidate surrogates, and ecological shelters to breed up and set loose revenant versions of extinct animals: the heath hen, the passenger pigeon, the mastodon. "Rewilding" reifies and imposes a fantasy ecology, prelapsarian and romantic, in which humans are either absent or themselves wild, *heimlich*, fully and impossibly at home.[6]

In place of rewilding, I want to renew an older term, now stale with familiarity: *bewilderment*, which mingles wildness with precarity, mystery, exile beyond the edges of norms and qualities. Samuel Johnson, the great English dictionary-maker, defined bewilderment as the condition of being "lost in pathless places . . . confound (ed) for want of a plain road."[7] It is a condition that arises at the edges, along the hedgerows and fences, in the wastes between towns—the regions which *Ailanthus* appropriates, darkens, bewilders in its flourishing. Bewilderment is the condition of the trickster, the habitat of Hermes, god of the in-between, the feral muse. And in our world of median strips and breezeways, of viaducts and vacant lots, this ferality and bewilderment are the growth habit, the phenology, the lifeway, and the species-being of *Ailanthus*. Through bewilderment—losing ourselves in the trees' pathless abundance—perhaps we can find the garden within the tree, the wild within the domesticated, the feral within the tame.

PART TWO

GARDEN AND FOREST

In the tree museum

We are back in the Arboretum—an abundance far from pathless, a cozy landscape of groves and copses and green slopes spilling open for the walker like a glossy magazine. A broad path of asphalt unwinds lazily before us, running some hundreds of yards before making an abrupt turn to climb into hills of lilacs beyond. To the left, a line of trees enfolds a low meadow, beyond which traffic on the Arborway goes shushing past, a white-noise horizon marking the limits of the urban. Before us, turned as we are now toward the meadow, stands an especially stately tree, a tall, spreading, sublimely vasiform *Ailanthus*. Here as with its kin elsewhere, the tree is in midsummer flower—and this specimen (for a specimen is what it is) displays its crop of vibrant red inflorescences. Dense plantings of sumac enclose a circular expanse of springy turf, surrounding and embowering the tree, furnishing a foundation to frame and emphasize its ruddy, spouting height.

Mounted on the speckled gray trunk there is a small black placard, emblazoned with a bit of sans-serif text, which reads as follows:

Ailanthus altissima
f. *erythrocarpa*
Form of Tree of Heaven
Native to China
SIMAROUBACEAE
695-80'B

Discreet and minimalist, these placards nonetheless remind us that the Arboretum is a living collection—a kind of museum or zoo for trees. For the casual visitor, the Arboretum is 285 acres of hills and fields softened by foliage and leaf-litter; it's the perfumed spring of the Lilac Collection, where tens of thousands of Bostonians gather to picnic on Mother's Day; the timbered glades of Hemlock Hill, with its grove of towering conifers now recovering from the ravages of the woody adelgid; the surprisingly sublime *bonsai* collection, with its wizened spruce and maples in miniature, some of them dating back to the eighteenth century; the Explorer's Garden on Bussey Hill, with its imperial booty of woody, leafy creatures from exotic locales. As a walk through the Arboretum unspools such sensory delights and contemplative vistas, it also offers spatialized argument about the biodiversity of woody plants of the northern hemisphere.

Folded into this landscape, then, inscribed and encoded into the plantings themselves and the signs and tags that mark and name them, are several ways of *doing* and *thinking* trees—habits of mind, perceptual and epistemic reflexes, some of which cut across our paradigm of the wild and the domesticated, the tame and the feral (while others exceed or transcend or ignore these collocations of qualities altogether). There is the tree as it has been done by biology, ecology, botany: the siting of the thousands of trees at the Arboretum follows a plan based on the Bentham-Hooker system, a nineteenth-century classification scheme for seed-bearing plants (and more will be said later about such taxonomies, their dark abundance of unglimpsed possibilities, and the arborescent forms by which we imagine and manipulate them). The botanical tree is also indexed by the placard described above, which offers an account of the tree in terms of the taxonomic family into which it's been sorted.

Ailanthus's family of trees, Simaroubaceae, gathers together a cohort of species that mostly thrive in the tropical south in both the eastern and western hemispheres. In this community, *Ailanthus*, native to temperate China, is an outlier. But it shares with the far-flung tribe characteristics salient to botanists. "The species from this family," according to a recent review essay in the *Revista Brasiliera de Farmacognosia* (2014), "have alternate compound or complete leafs, not punctuate, with or without thorns. Its flowers are, generally, placed together in axial inflorescences, showing free or fused sepals, free petals, stamens in double of the number of the petals, filaments usually with appendix." In addition to these anatomical markers, botany counts and organizes qualities that take shape in physiological, biochemical, and genetic terms; the authors of the *Revista* article call the family "a promising source of bioactive molecules with remarkable research potential." In some places, the authors call these "quassinoids" (also alkaloids, triterpenes, steroids, coumarins, anthraquinones, flavonoids) and "secondary metabolites"; elsewhere, they're content to term them "bitter substances."[1]

The characteristic quassinoid produced by *Ailanthus* goes by the name "ailanthone," which inhibits the growth of other plants. The rumor of this substance, said to act as an herbicide to native plants and approved horticultural varieties, is one of the chief reasons that *Ailanthus* is reviled by gardeners, although it's a capacity in which the Tree of Heaven is far from unique. Indeed the domain of "allelopathic chemicals" produced by plants of all kinds is vast, and still vastly mysterious, although the effect (not in *Ailanthus*, but in pigweed's relationship with alfalfa) was noted by Theophrastus in 300 BCE. Such chemicals are produced as "secondary metabolites"—substances that are by products of metabolism and not strictly necessary for the maintenance of a plant's physiology. Yet thanks to the intrinsic messiness of photosynthesis, plants throw off a vast array of bioproducts, some of which produce startling and ramifying results in interaction with the world.

The family noted on the *Ailanthus* specimen's placard also exists as the "cohors SIMARUBEÆ" in the Bentham-Hooker system, although subsumed to a different set of higher orders there than in the regnant taxonomic system. That latter system—which takes shape as the cascade of classes, orders, and families familiar from high-school biology—is administered by the International Botanical Congress, a standards body and deliberative organization drawing its membership from the international community of plant scientists. Their deliberations guide the editorial program of the *International Code of Nomenclature for Algae, Fungi, and Plants* (ICN). This publication serves as the botanical Napoleonic Code, codifying and regulating the scientific description of plants; it dates its scientific pedigree back to 1753, the year that

Linnaeus's *Species Plantarum* was published, establishing a continuity with the Linnaean tradition even as it supersedes and effaces all prior versions of that system (and competing versions, such as Bentham-Hooker's—which nonetheless find trickling life in places like the Arboretum, thanks to custom and the long lives of hard-to-move trees). On the placard we also have the Linnaean genus and specific epithet (to which in this case a further appellation, *erythrocarpa*, is appended, denominating by reference to the Greek words for "red" and "seed" a further-distinguishable form contained within the fuzzy set of the species). Breaking the centered symmetry, parked to the left in smaller type, the accession number of this particular tree, a formula that gives it a place in the collection, a history, with beginning dates and (unknown but implacable) and end point as well. This accession number coordinates the individual organism with the collection as a whole, assigning it a place in the imaginal assemblage of the Arboretum that complements, but is not identical with, its geographical location on the grounds. The database home of this specimen of the Tree of Heaven, the metadata-domicile it inhabits, looks like this:

Ailanthus altissima forma erythrocarpa

Accession number: 695-80
Accession date: 24 Jun 1980
Received as: division

Provenance:
Cultivated material from United States   MA

Locality: Route 128 along Charles River, on northeast shore

Collector(s) and/or collection number(s): Del Tredici, P. S. N.

Source: P. Del Tredici, Arnold Arb.

Living plants of this accession
Individual Plant - Location (grid or other) - Quadrant (if applicable)
B   8   SW

This is the entry for 695-80 in BG-Base, the specialized bota-nical database in which the Arboretum records the accession and vital records (germination, division, grafting, pruning, blossoming, and eventual senescence) of the more than 70,000 plants that have comprised the living collection over the Arboretum's history. This database entry also coordinates the individual tree with a record of publication: specifically, the *Bibliography of Cultivated Trees and Shrubs Hardy in the Cooler Temperate Regions of the Northern Hemisphere.*[2] This entry, indexed by hyperlink from the record transcribed above, points toward a book in the library, a place on the shelf, from which the long list of books on *Ailanthus* and its vast army of confreres and conspecifics is rendered discoverable. We go from placard to record to library shelf in a few keystrokes, traversing tap-a-tap doorways that hinge successively on accession number, Linnaean binomial, and geographic location, each hinge articulating space with time, discourse with silence, knowledge with a dark, unknown abundance.

The database tells many stories. As my colleague, Yanni Loukissas, explains, "Data have been woven through the development and use of the Harvard's living collection since its founding in 1872. . . . Housing databases of both the living and the dead, the Arboretum is a place in which being is a function of information."[3] Now at Georgia Tech, Loukissas joined our group's work in the Arboretum in 2013, bringing to bear both his training as a science-studies scholar and his design-driven understanding of data. He spent a couple of years looking into the ways of the Arboretum's collection—which includes not only thousands of living trees planted throughout 281 acres, but drawers and folders of dried herbaria specimens, repositories of seeds, and tissue samples frozen or otherwise preserved, and archival materials such as maps and field notes. It might seem as though, at a place like the Arnold Arboretum, trees *become* data, are *reduced to* data, transformed into the mute traces of laws and systems beyond their ken. But objects are insistent, and living ones especially; and through Loukissas's work on metadata, we learn that trees in the Arboretum take voice and learn to speak in a broken smattering of dialects across index cards, herbarium sheets, and the slick keys where data take digital form.

Through close study of the collections database, Loukissas learned that the 70,000 trees that have been planted at the Arboretum over its history arrived in distinct waves, which tell stories of the Arboretum's role in botany, in environmental science, and in the city of Boston. The Arboretum began its institutional life in the 1870s through a marriage of science and landscape architecture; the study of trees and other living things on the one hand, and the design of parks and public spaces on the other, were both undergoing transformation. Botany was still in the midst of the Darwinian moment, and the systems of classification advanced out of Enlightenment precepts of order and rationality were being transformed into stories of the history of life.

Parks, meanwhile, were in the midst of a transformation from aristocratic luxuries into Victorian tools of social and personal improvement. This shift was symbolized, if not solely enacted, by one figure above all: Frederick Law Olmsted, designer of New York's Central Park and the pioneer of landscape architecture. The Arboretum is integral to Olmsted's design for the Emerald Necklace; within its bounds, his vision of parks as green social batteries, repositories of restorative vistas and tree-softened terrain, met Arboretum founder Charles Sprague Sargent's desire to tell the story of woody life's unfolding.[4]

Olmsted's designs weren't in the first instance about natural history, however, but the city and its problems. For Olmsted, parks could mask the city's jagged and smoky skyline, taking salarymen and wage-earners into a virtual countryside far from workaday concerns, disclosing, through their winding, woody paths and suddenly opening swards of turf and shrub, pastorals of clement repose. The challenge wasn't merely aesthetic, however, but material, mechanical—and trees were key to solving the problem. "Air is disinfected by sunlight and foliage," he remarked in an address at Boston's Lowell Institute in 1870, not long before the opening of the Arboretum:

> Foliage also acts mechanically to purify the air by screening it. Opportunity and inducement to escape at frequent intervals from the confined and vitiated air of the commercial quarter, and to supply the lungs with air screened and purified by trees, and recently acted on by sunlight, together with the opportunity and inducement to escape from conditions requiring vigilance, wariness, and activity toward other men—if these could be supplied economically, our problem would be solved.

Integral to this vision, Olmsted later argues, is the desire for "depth of wood . . . not only for comfort in hot weather, but to *completely shut out the city* from our landscapes" (emphasis mine). Olmsted wasn't anti urban; he was instead sensitive to the ways in which cities were undergoing rapid transformation and growth in the nineteenth century, spreading rapidly both horizontally and vertically, mingling residential and industrial districts chaotically.

Olmsted was struck by how the modern city, under these conditions, used and misused trees:

Trees are planted in the space assigned for sidewalks, where at first, while they are saplings, and the vicinity is rural or suburban, they are not much in the way, but where, as they grow larger, and the vicinity becomes more urban, they take up more and more space, while space is more required for passage. . . . Thousands and tens of thousands are planted every year in a manner and under conditions as nearly certain as possible to kill them outright, or to so lessen their vitality as to prevent their natural and beautiful development, and to cause premature decrepitude. . . . If by rare fortune they are suffered to become beautiful, they still stand subject to be condemned to death at any time, as obstructions in the highway.[5]

More than mere foliage, trees in Olmsted's city should become aesthetic, sanitary, and civic forces. In the Arboretum, this gentle civic vision was given an education spin, as trees were asked to teach of life as well. Such was the ambition of Charles Sprague Sargent, the horticulturalist who served as the Arboretum's founding director. The site's rolling landscape, however, while conducive to Olmsted's rugged pastoralism, frustrated the pedagogical clarity Sargent desired. "The difficulties of making a proper plan for laying out the Arboretum have always appeared very great to me," he wrote. "The site, while offering exceptional beauties, perhaps, for a public park, offers exceptional topographical difficulties for the object to which it is to be devoted; namely, a museum, in which as many living specimens as possible were to find their appropriate positions."[6] In its design, ultimately, the Arnold Arboretum struck a bargain: its swooping roads and unfolding hills would disclose not only bucolic odes but—gently, subtly, with a prosody fully recognizable only to its cognoscenti—the kin relations of the woody plants as well.

Such was the overriding ambition of the Arboretum in its first few decades. And thus Olmsted's landscape aesthetic was made foundational and subservient to the scientific work of the facility—which, at the height of nineteenth-century colonial imperialism, was expressed through an expeditionary, acquisitive methodology that extended to collecting institutions of all kinds. In 1816, the friezes of the Athenian Parthenon famously entered the collection of the British Museum under the title of the "Elgin Marbles," renamed for the Earl who had laid dubious claim to them. In the early 1840s, the United States Exploring Expedition had circled the globe, returning with a 50,000-specimen herbarium and a vast store of animal specimens and cultural artifacts to enrich the newly founded Smithsonian Institution in Washington. The American Museum of Natural History swelled with the knowledge-producing treasure of botanists, ethnologists, entomologists, geologists—the disciplines splaying and branching spasmodically as science professionalized. Across the Western world, collections in the mid-nineteenth century burgeoned with colonial booty collected in the name of science—and the Arboretum was a product of that era, its scientists climbing into the valleys of

Qin-dynasty China in search of trees that could tell the story of trees with salience and esoteric beauty.

The problems of this acquisitive, encyclopedic, universalizing kind of collection-building are by now well-rehearsed; they've seen effective critiques mounted by Michel Foucault and others. My favorite critique of the supposed fixity of things comes from the poet W. H. Auden, who in his poem "Objects" suggests that "if shapes can so to their own edges keep, no separation proves a being bad."[7] The separation of objects into discrete data points is one of the supreme fictions of the museum. For as we know, objects do not to their edges keep; the meaning of Periclean-Age friezes, for instances, have proven much more difficult to police than Thomas Bruce, 11th Lord Elgin, believed when he had them cut from the marble matrix of the ruined Parthenon.

In living collections like the Arboretum, the problem is heightened and compounded, for trees perform this borderlessness with implacable biotic zeal. By the early twentieth century, the cosmopolitan camp followers of mostly Asian trees in the Arboretum collection—the insects, fungi, and invasive vascular plants carried in the fibrous tissues of trees and shrubs—had migrated readily from the picturesque confines of the Emerald Necklace to make their presence felt in nurseries, gardens, and North America's rapidly vanishing woodlands. The problem of the invasive species was less the trace of any moral character inherent in a weedy, feral creature itself than it was a telling by-product of a restless and acquisitive age. In the mid-twentieth century, the newly established US Department of Agriculture came down hard on the Arboretum, forbidding the institution's import of new specimens for several decades.

During this time, the Arboretum reinterpreted its mission, closely aligning itself with Olmsted's legacy of the health and mental hygiene to be found in parklands. The Arboretum became a center for horticultural knowledge production, privileging the design affordances of trees over their ability to tell stories about the tree of life. The Arboretum's focus on the exotic took a turn away from bare life toward artifactual ways of doing trees, emphasizing the extraordinary effects achieved by nurseries through the crafts of cultivation. It wasn't until its centennial in the early 1970s, as Yanni Loukissas reports, that the Arboretum renewed its commitment to exploration in botanical science, ecology, and genetic research. Scientists there began expanding their fieldwork, Loukissas observes, "through new relationships with institutions in Asia and reframed around the emergent and imperative questions of global climate change."

These shifts in emphasis and interest, Loukissas shows, are both revealed by and hidden in the database. His essay on the Arboretum is a remarkable hybrid—part prose article, part data visualization—that explores and explicates some of the stories that trees try to tell through the Arboretum's metadata. In the left column, an array of pixels represents some 70,000 accessions of trees and shrubs—all of the organisms acquired by the Arboretum over the course of its history (which is to say, all those deemed fit for designation as specimens in the collection—for as we've seen at sites like Bussey Brook Meadow, trees can live in the Arboretum without joining the collection, visible and tangible as organisms, and yet invisible as data). Most of the trees documented in the database are dead and gone, long ago converted into mulch (which ebbs and flows in a depot at the edge of the grounds—a small, room-like spent granite quarry where piles of pulped and chipped wood rise and fall, steaming from the heat of their own fermentation). But in the database, the living and the dead have an equal footing as data points in a portrait of the Arboretum as a collecting institution. Even as the trees are (nearly) all present there, the stories they tell are largely reduced to a single narrative, that of accessioning, identifying, tracking provenance—which tends to supersede or efface the countless individual, peculiar stories of trees' coming and becoming.

Loukissas tangles with these elisions and erasures in the prose portion of his essay, where he turns to our friend Peter Del Tredici for examples of arborescent forms of life the metadata have made invisible. During a visit to the Arboretum's "Explorer's Garden," where especially striking and exotic specimens, mostly from Asia, shelter beneath the brow of a hill, Del Tredici described his special fondness for the plants there. "I've got a lot of direct connection to a lot of these plants," Loukissas records Del Tredici saying. "That little plant, *Torreya grandis*, I collected in China in 1989. So a lot of these are like, my offspring." The *Torreya grandis*, sometimes called the "Chinese nutmeg yew," sports yew-like foliage with flat needles, sticky with gum, hanging palm-like fronds. Also like the yew and a few other gymnosperms counted as conifers, *T. grandis* doesn't bear a shingled cone but instead produces a flesh-covered pit called an aril, similar to those produced by flowering plants. In this aspect it isn't unique—you've likely seen the berrylike arils of the yew, for instance, festooning boxy, trimmed hedges and rangy dooryard bushes, where they fluoresce amid the shadowed needles with a wanton, raspberry-pink vividness. Trees are playful mimics when it comes to their sexual parts; flowering plants have copied conifers, too: the small, winged seeds of *Platycarya strobilacea* from Asia take flight from a fruiting structure, called an "infructescence" by botanists, which is strikingly cone-like in structure.[8] The flesh of the yew's aril is moist, sticky, and sickly sweet, and there is at the bottom a tiny porthole where a bullet-shaped seed not much larger than a pencil eraser peers out. The yew aril is edible, but the seed—like the rest of the yew, from needle to root—is quite toxic. Songbirds delight in these yew-berries, consuming them whole and passing the seeds unprocessed through their guts. Today, we mostly do the yew as a woody shrub and an edge planting; but yews in the West have a long history of entanglement with humans: their springy wood was traditionally used in archer's bows, and long-lived individual trees are often found in the yards of medieval churches, speaking to some combination of practical and sacred uses for the tree dating to pre-Christian times. Celtic tribes were recorded poisoning themselves with yew rather than surrendering to Caesar, and Yggdrasil, the world-tree of Norse myth, from which Odin hangs himself in sacrifice to discover the secret of written language, though once imagined as an ash, is now thought by some scholars to have been a yew. Found throughout Western Europe, churchyard yews are among the oldest living things in the world, some of them surely dating to pre-Christian times. This may speak to lost sacral meanings of the yew, as early European churches often were built at sites holy to Celtic and Germanic tribes. Instead, it may reflect the yew's useful toxicity, with trees cultivated to dissuade herdsmen from pasturing sheep and cattle in church burial grounds. This latter use likely explains the origins of the yew's use in edge plantings, trimmed and trained into shrubby hedges instead of the broad, dense, multi-trunked arbors it prefers to form. We no longer make use of the yew for its poison, however, but we do value the color of its uncanny arils, a brightness that brings the chattering of winter birds.

The arils of *T. grandis* are larger than those of the yew, and fully enclosed—tiny, pistachio-sized gourds striated with cool tones of green; the seeds, which look like a cross between nutmeg and almond, are edible (and prized as a snack). The *Torreya* in the Explorers' Garden were raised from seeds found by Peter Del Tredici in a Chinese market; as Loukissas reports, this provenance examples the kind of strange, hybrid journey taken by many Arboretum trees:

The acquisition date of the *Torreya grandis* and Del Tredici's association with it are duly noted in the Arboretum's database. . . . Del Tredici is identified as a "collector," not as a "progenitor" or even "breeder" as his statement would suggest—this, despite the fact that he is responsible for the reproduction of the plant in the Boston region. Indeed, the term "collector" speaks of the scientist-and-specimen relationship between Del Tredici and the plant, neither of his role as a teacher, nor of the more nurturing association between Del Tredici the horticulturalist and the organism he has cultivated. The last of these is more in line with his own intimate way of identifying with the *Torreya grandis* as an "offspring" in this particular moment.[9]

The collections database can offer a narrative of the ebb and flow of acquisitions. But it doesn't necessarily reveal the full web of relations among trees, humans, and the ways we have of knowing, manipulating, and addressing them—of *doing* trees. The metadata may seek to describe, Loukissas argues, "without fully explaining how plants like the *Torreya* are deracinated: figuratively torn up by the roots and redefined in a new social and cultural context. . . . Del Tredici likens the 'raw data' to seeds. When a seed won't germinate, there are innumerable possible reasons. 'Unless you know how to interpret the behavior of the seed, it's just non-data.'"

As I sit here, cogitating over the order and disclosure of qualities botanical, horticultural, material, apparent, and phenomenal; as I consider the complementarity of these well-placed and petted norms and truths with the baroque mystery of the many unglimpsed facets of the trees, I look up to gaze out the window, and a honey locust up the street—its canopy even with me in my fourth-floor office—seems to stick a vagrant bough into the passing, sun-whipped summer breeze. The bough shakes with ponderous vigor—I can't help thinking that it's imploring me to plow on, although of course it's only responding to the sprung priorities of cambium and heartwood, the tangle of gravity with the fugal expression of leaves and branches.

Through these hinges, other ways of thinking and doing the tree are brought into association. There is the horticultural dimension: how the tree is performed as an object of attention in the gardener's imagination, how it takes up its place in the practice of the arborist. Let's return to our specimen Tree of Heaven, *A. altissima erthythrocarpa*, member of the Simuraboecaeae. Its accession number, emblazoned on the placard, is 695-80. The tree arrived as the 695th acquisition of the year 1980 at the Arboretum—with this observation of mere chronology the accession number also situates the organism in a program of planting and cultivation as well as curatorial and scientific attention. We also see that the tree was received as a "division"—meaning it was a cutting from a plant already flourishing elsewhere. And with its "locality," we learn something crucial and compelling about its provenance: the cutting was taken from a tree growing along Route 128, the section of Interstate 95 that makes an open parenthesis around the Boston area, bracketing it on the west. The shoulders of the highway are a vector for *Ailanthus*, which flourishes in the programmatic neglect of the state highway department, its tropical fronds churning in the unceasing wind kicked up by semi-trailers and onrushing commuters. Of this sordid and feral origin, the database record is a modest witness, making a record that leads to the margin of mystery with perfect equanimity, empirical and unprepossessing.

Trees in the Arboretum *act* as data in multiple ways at once: as individual specimens in specific microclimates, thriving and dying as organisms; distributed in abstract spatiality across the 281 acres of the Arboretum; expressed in the relations of the Bentham-Hooker taxonomic system; and in the database, ordered as fungible records of equal weight arrayed in tables. The tree learns to speak these peculiar domestic idioms of the human, coordinating and cross-referencing the spatial with the paradigmatic, grid and quadrant with accession number, index card, and database entry. Other instruments of scientific bureaucracy collate with these systems as well: dried and pressed fronds and stems in the herbarium; files and boxes of papers in the archive; books and albums of photographs in the library.

As with *Torreya grandis*, the database's anodyne descriptors efface the intimate and embedded details of this particular Tree of Heaven's acquisition. "The director said he'd seen an *Ailanthus* along the highway with really red blooms," Peter Del Tredici told me a couple of summers ago, "and he told me to go and get it. That's how we ended up with it." Since Kyle and I first toured Bussey Brook Meadow with him, Peter has retired as senior researcher at the Arboretum, although he remains a lecturer on landscape at Harvard's Graduate School of Design. A plant-worker with both horticultural and scientific training, Del Tredici is a rare specimen himself. His career at the Arboretum spanned nearly forty years, during which time he went from pinching and pruning the *bonsai* collection, trimming and transplanting flowering shrubs, and managing other tasks of the gardener and the arborist, to traveling the world to research the biology of northern temperate trees as a research botanist. Peter's cutting, 695-80, has grown into a tall, splendidly formed tree, which does much to efface its feral origins as a highway invasive, where it began as another seed whipped along in the slipstream of big rigs and motorcycles, following the roads and railways to spread with its kind up and down the Northeast Corridor, flourishing in cloverleaf copses, using off-ramps and overpass embankments to gain footholds in wayside neighborhoods. Which is not to say that such an origin troubles Del Tredici. Indeed, it seems to give him no small amount of pleasure— Del Tredici can't mention *Ailanthus* without having his voice drawn into a drawl by a slow-blooming smile. For he's also the principal investigator and ecological guiding spirit at Bussey Brook Meadow, where that provisional grove of tall, lithe *Ailanthus* make their stand on the landfill mesa overlooking the reeds. It was Del Tredici who convinced the Arboretum leadership to let him manage Bussey Brook as an "urban wild," a hot zone for the peculiar, cosmopolitan biodiversity that makes up the little-known, often-reviled green backdrop of the city.

The management plan for the meadow expresses the paradoxes of this situation in neutralizing terms: "The Arnold Arboretum will continue to *maintain* the land in the Bussey Brook Meadow as an 'urban wild,'" it states, "rather than as an *active* part of the botanical collection" (my emphases). There's a neat brace of contradictions at work here: a *maintained wildness* strictly cordoned off from an *active collection*. To be "active" in this curatorial sense, a tree must be accessioned, fixed by the hinges of the database to place, patrimony, and publication; what is active in this case of course is not the tree (which is not to say that trees are inactive, as it should by now be clear), but the curatorial program of the Arboretum, producing knowledge, doing and doing with trees in special ways. *Taming* trees. (The horticulturalist domesticates; the curator tames.) In the meadow, by contrast, the Arboretum maintains a wildness (that quality which, one is wont to suggest, normally and normatively marks that beyond the reach of maintenance). What is maintained? Arboretum staff repair stone walls and iron gates; they install and maintain signs and benches; they prune overhanging trees dangerous to passersby, remove woody vines threatening the viability of desired mature trees, and clear debris obstructing the flow of the brook. Interventions are described precisely: "The mowing width has been mapped using GPS technology to the nearest decimeter," the charter insists, "and shall be followed as such" to avoid "compromising the integrity of future data."[10] So even here, outside the curated collection of trees in the Arboretum across the road, it is *data*—or conditions productive to certain kinds of data, at any rate—which are to be cultivated and maintained. For all the careful measurement, however, the borders of the meadow and its zones of life are slippery, weedy, and unstable, subject to negotiation by human and nonhuman. The trees, vines, and shrubs of the meadow stand in feral relation to this maintenance, arguing with its disciplinary idiom, gnawing at its margins.

None of Bussey Brook's *Ailanthus* are accessioned as specimens. Indeed, no trees of any species in the meadow are recognized as part of the collection; instead, they thrive there as a population, studied in community: branches wound tightly with bittersweet vine, combating with the cottonwoods for light and soil. (And data are gathered about them in this condition, to be sure; a team of graduate students is tracking the progress of Bussey Brook Meadow under Peter's leadership.) Here, another aspect of the tree-as-organism is done: one distinct from, but overlapping with, that practiced in the Arboretum proper; the tree is regarded as a rhizomatic object, a body without organs, spreading emergently as flow or force, suckering and sprouting, rising to fill the gaps. As dramatis personae in an ecological tableau, *Ailanthus* and cottonwood, rank weed and stout tree, vie with one another atop the mesa, acting out the morality play of native and invasive.

In spring, motes of cottonwood seed-fluff drift through sun-slatted air which, when the brush is broken by a walker, carries also the faint rank musk of the Tree of Heaven. Here and there, middens of cardboard and discarded clothing flatten the forest duff; in a clearing torn open by a great fallen cottonwood, a new crop of *Ailanthus* seedlings raise their lacy heads, look to the gaps, and grow. So *Ailanthus* find space to flourish in Bussey Brook, unaccessioned, watched. And meanwhile at the edges of the Arboretum, where its granite-block walls line Olmsted's serpentine parkways and the manicured trees nod at the edges of the neighborhoods, the feral *Ailanthus* rise, a rank tangle of seedlings and young, wood-bearing trees, some of them the offspring of the specimen tree nestled deep within the Arboretum's cultivated grounds. Domesticated, Wild, Tame, and Feral: ways of doing trees, and trees doing the human.

From *Ailanthus* to apple

To complicate the banquet we've set with wild and domesticated, tame and feral, let's introduce another tree to the table—a tree, indeed, from which we're inclined to eat. On first reflection, few trees could seem so different from wanton *Ailanthus* than the apple, the paragon of arboreal domesticity. And yet *Malus*, too, can express itself ferally. Henry David Thoreau appraised the apple's juggling of wild and domesticated qualities in terms congenial to our consideration of ferality, noting that Pliny identified that "of trees there are some which are altogether wild (*sylvestres*), song more, civilized (*urbaniores*)." Thoreau continues:

> Theophrastus includes the apple among the last; and, indeed, it is in this sense the most civilized of all trees. It is as harmless as a dove, as beautiful as a rose, and as valuable as flocks and herds. It has been longer cultivated than any other, and so is more humanized; and who knows but, like the dog, it will at length be no longer traceable to its wild original? It migrates with man, like the dog and horse and cow: first, perchance from Greece to Italy, thence to England: thence to America; and our Western emigrant is still marching steadily toward the setting sun with the seeds of the apple in his pocket, or perhaps a few young trees strapped to his load.[1]

Thoreau's keen appreciation for the apple as a fellow traveler in the natural history of humankind presages E. J. Salisbury's formulation of weedy ecology—a migratory bent that is particularly notable in connection with such problematically denominated qualities as "native" and "invasive," wild and domesticated. As we have seen, the species decried by ecology as "invasive" are our fellow travelers—part of the vast, glimmering, herbaceous shadow that followed us out of the garden or out of Africa and into the fruitful fields of the Levant, east Asia, the Andean highlands, wherever agriculture first took root. This ancient story was reprised in the coming of the apple to North America—although there were varieties of wild crabapple at large in North America, with their bitter, tiny fists of fruit, the apple that thrives today is an introduced tree, arriving as a harbinger and enabler of the Age of Discovery, arriving accompanied by people who bore along with its scions a belief in a fall from grace in the terrible discovery of the Tree of Knowledge. And as Thoreau describes, this preeminent orchard and garden tree escapes the normative stipulations of this colonizing culture, finding its feral way quickly in the new Eden—and finds it, moreover, in company with many other creatures:

> Not only the Indian, but many indigenous insects, birds, and quadrupeds, welcomed the apple-tree to these shores. The tent-caterpillar saddled her eggs on the very first twig that was formed, and it has since shared her affections

with the wild cherry; and the canker-worm also in a measure abandoned the elm to feed on it. As it grew apace, the blue-bird, robin, cherry-bird, king-bird, and many more, came with haste and built their nests and warbled in its boughs, and so became orchard-birds, and multiplied more than ever. It was an era in the history of their race. The downy woodpecker found such a savory morsel under its bark, that he perforated it in a ring, quite round the tree, before he left it,—a thing which he had never done before, to my knowledge. It did not take the partridge long to find out how sweet its buds were, and every winter eve she flew, and still flies, from the wood, to pluck them, much to the farmer's sorrow. The rabbit, too, was not slow to learn the taste of its twigs and bark; and when the fruit was ripe, the squirrel half-rolled, half-carried it to his hole; and even the musquash crept up the bank from the brook at evening, and greedily devoured it, until he had worn a path in the grass there; and when it was frozen and thawed, the crow and the jay were glad to taste it occasionally. The owl crept into the first apple-tree that became hollow, and fairly hooted with delight, finding it just the place for him; so settling down into it, he has remained there ever since.[2]

Although Thoreau richly appreciates the community of orchards, long cultivated, that patterns the townlands west of Boston, it is the tree-escapees who capture his fancy and suit his back-lot-wandering ways:

Going up the side of a cliff about the first of November, I saw a vigorous young apple-tree, which, planted by birds or cows, had shot up amid the rocks and open woods there, and had now much fruit on it, uninjured by the frosts, when all cultivated apples were gathered. It was a rank wild growth, with many green leaves on it still, and made an impression of thorniness. The fruit was hard and green, but looked as if it would be palatable in the winter. Some was dangling, on the twigs, but more half-buried in the wet leaves under the tree, or rolled far down the hill amid the rocks. The owner knows nothing of it. The day was not observed when it first blossomed, nor when it first bore fruit, unless by the chickadee. There was no dancing, on the green beneath it in its honor, and now there is no hand to pluck its fruit,—which is only gnawed by squirrels, as I perceive. It has done double duty,—not only borne this crop, but each twig has grown a foot into the air. And this is such fruit! bigger than many berries, we must admit, and carried home will be sound and palatable next spring. What care I for Iduna's apples so long as I can get these?[3]

Thoreau's apple chooses its own way in the world: it "emulates man's independence and enterprise. It is not simply carried, as I have said, but, like him, to some extent, it has migrated to this New World, and is even, here and there, making its way amid the aboriginal trees; just as the ox and dog and horse sometimes run wild and maintain themselves." So while

Thoreau called his essay "Wild Apples," it should be clear to us by now that the trees he's writing about are feral. They make their bargains with gravity, wind, and the browsing ways of wandering cattle that browse them close to the ground.

> Thus cut down annually, it does not despair; but, putting forth two short twigs for every one cut off, it spreads out low along the ground in the hollows or between the rocks, growing more stout and scrubby, until it forms, not a tree as yet, but a little pyramidal, stiff, twiggy mass, almost as solid and impenetrable as a rock. Some of the densest and most impenetrable clumps of bushes that I have ever seen, as well on account of the closeness and stubbornness of their branches as of their thorns, have been these wild-apple scrubs. They are more like the scrubby fir and black spruce on which you stand, and sometimes walk, on the tops of mountains, where cold is the demon they contend with, than anything else. No wonder they are prompted to grow thorns at last, to defend themselves against such foes. In their thorniness, however, there is no malice, only some malic acid.[4]

Thoreau is keenly attentive to the many forms taken by apple trees, and to the stories they tell. Trees are always inspiring our attention to form. The forms of trees also inspired Johann Wolfgang von Goethe, who found in the rhymes and designs of botanical form a powerful critique of the experimental and analytic modes that had come to dominate scientific thinking in the eighteenth century. For Goethe and many who came after him, this attention is especially enlivened by the tree's slow, patient expression of form over time. "The growth of trees," Del Tredici writes, "is totally different from that of vertebrate animals, which tend to reach their full developmental potential relatively early in life, and then maintain themselves in the mature stage for as long as possible. To put it another way, animals are closed and entire in their development while trees are open and expansive."[5] This openness and expansiveness, Del Tredici writes, is the consequence of the tissue that is responsible for tree growth, the meristem. This embryonic tissue exists throughout the life of a tree, ready to produce new differentiated cells for the various constituent tissues of the tree: the cork or bark, the vascular cambium, the root, and the shoot or growth tip. A tree is sheathed in meristematic tissue; "a gigantic cylindrical meristem . . . outlines the periphery of the entire tree. . . . A direct consequence of the meristematic structure of trees is that everything that has ever happened to them over the course of their long lives is embedded in the very fiber of their being, which is to say, the structure of their wood." The unfolding form of a tree over the course of its life is a living expression of an ongoing dialogue between its internal physiological processes and the external assaults and offerings of its environment.

Del Tredici credits Goethe's attention to the forms of plants, or morphology, as a critical perspective on trees as objects—and one not taken by the mainstream life sciences in the modern era. In his critical encounter with modern science, Goethe paid great attention to the morphology of plants, finding the taxonomic abstractions of the emergent science of botany alienating, liable to draining life of life. The Linnaean classification system, for Goethe, operated by sorting plants into unbridgeable provinces of mechanism and form, denying plant life—all of nature, the world in its entirety—its deep-foundationed spirit and unity. In contrast to Linnaeus, for whom anatomical differences were markers of unbridgeable differences declared and disciplined by a divine order, for Goethe the diversity of forms were like utterances in a long-running discourse, fluid and poetic inventions in a single song. In the diversity of botanical forms, Goethe sought the original, the primal, the prototype plant—*Die Urpflanze*—which takes shape not as a primordial, extinct ancestor but as an idea, a sort of romantic notion held in common by all plant life. There is in Goethe's science an idealism, a Platonism; but where Socrates had put the value and meaning of the world in those immaterial and unattainable ideas, for Goethe the guiding forms were more lightly held, less ideas than ideologies. What counted, what was important, was their expression in resonating, harmonic diversity of unfolding forms—with form not as plan or model, but a kind of dance, a thing that happens unfoldingly in space and time.

This peculiar notion of prototype, too, takes shape in the tree's expression of reiterative growth: in response to assaults and opportunities of wind, light, and competition, the tree will repeatedly express its basic structural model.

There is a poetry to this unfolding, a kind of fugal iteration of theme and variation, which make trees powerful memory repositories both for their own life histories and the world in which they grow. "When leaves divide, or when they advance from their original state to diversity," Goethe observed, "they are striving towards greater perfection, in the sense that each leaf has the intention of becoming a branch, and each branch a tree."[6]

Goethe's practice of science eschewed the artifice and mise-en-scène of experimentation for the grounded intimacy of observation, a celebratory privileging of immersion in and immediate sensuous dialogue with things in the world. And while this approach to *natura naturans* (nature naturing) has been deprecated in modern scientific practice, it remains a perfectly salient and productive way to experience the world. Indeed, you can reliably orient yourself in a strange place by practicing Goethean attention to the stories told by trees: in the northern hemisphere, branches growing on the southern side of a tree will express themselves horizontally, lending the body of the tree an asymmetrical profile, with dense, vertical branches to the north and grasping, open-armed boughs to the south. Tristan Gooley calls this "the tick effect,"[7] an evocative way of naming the slowly unfolding rhythmic gestures of trees reaching out, hungry for light.

Pondering the tree's strange capacities—its reiterative growth, its perennially embryonic meristem, its morphological unity and expressiveness—Del Tredici (2002) makes an observation at once obvious and uncanny: "The shape of an individual tree is analogous to the personality of a human. . . . Everything that ever happens to a tree in the course of its long life is embedded in its form, even the little things that might have happened to the tree when it was just a sapling. The body language of trees speaks not only to the influence of the past in the present, but also to the promise of the future." We find our capacity for such personality-making in cognition, encapsulated in brains and extended through our social bodies; for the tree, this thinking takes place in wood, in growth, and in form. Although they're sessile, we can see how plants move, interact, and even collaborate and compete with one another, very slowly in time. But in addition to these anthropomorphic features, we should understand the tree's own arborescent ways of being, making, and saying. To Henry, the apple's ways speak most warmly to those humans who, like the trees, have cultivated the feral qualities:

> They belong to children as wild as themselves,—to certain active boys that I know—to the wild-eyed woman of the fields, to whom nothing comes amiss, who gleans after all the world,—and, moreover, to us walkers. We have met with them, and they are ours. These rights, long enough insisted upon, have come to be an institution in some old countries, where they have learned how to live.[8]

And yet this conversation is always on the verge of silence. With his customary, exasperating prescience, Henry imagines the end of the apple's feral commonwealth:

I fear that he who walks over these fields a century hence will not know the pleasure of knocking off wild apples. Ah, poor man, there are many pleasures which he will not know! Notwithstanding the prevalence of the Baldwin and the Porter, I doubt if so extensive orchards are set out to-day in my town as there were a century ago, when those vast straggling cider-orchards were planted, when men both ate and drank apples, when the pomace-heap was the only nursery, and trees cost nothing but the trouble of setting them out. Men could afford then to stick a tree by every wall-side and let it take its chance. I see nobody planting trees to-day in such out-of-the-way places, along the lonely roads and lanes, and at the bottom of dells in the wood. Now that they have grafted trees, and pay a price for them, they collect them into a plat by their houses, and fence them in—and the end of it all will be that we shall be compelled to look for our apples in a barrel.[9]

No drinker, Thoreau lays the blame for the feral apple's demise in part at the feet of the temperance movement. Apples, after all, were cultivated in large part for the production of hard cider, the most popular alcoholic beverage throughout nineteenth-century America. But he sees many other forces at work as well: the emergence of larger-scale, industrially minded cultivation, with grafting and fencing the emergent norm and "nobody planting trees in such out-of-the-way places . . . at the bottom of dells in the woods." Thoreau's observation seems to register a change in attitudes toward the land, one long under way in modern Europe and North America, and well advanced by Thoreau's time (when the fields around Concord had already been in continuous cultivation by Anglo-Americans for more than two hundred years, with gentler, yet still transformative, forms of use practiced by native North Americans for centuries before that). I wonder if Thoreau's parting shot at collecting orchards into "a plat by their houses, and fenc(ing) them in" isn't a quiet dig at his mentor and sponsor, Ralph Waldo Emerson, whose orchards and trees Thoreau tended for part-time pay. [10] After his death, Emerson said of Thoreau, that with his "energy and practical ability he seemed born for great enterprise and command"—and yet in the end, "instead of engineering for all America, he was captain of a huckleberry party."[11]

Feral apples of the kind Thoreau prized are indeed hard to find in eastern Massachusetts today; the orchards are measured out and fenced; corn-maze sprints and hayrides on the half-hour substitute for Henry's wild sauntering. *Ailanthus*, however, still finds its feral way, even near the petted preserve of Walden Wood; it flourishes along the rough embankments and caterpillar-churned earthworks along the old Cambridge-Concord Turnpike (today a newly re-widened Massachusetts Route 2). *Ailanthus* springs up in great, tropical bouquets around the Alewife MBTA station; its sprung fringes churn in the car-whipped wind that rounds the rotaries at Fresh Pond; its saplings crowd up through the cracks in the concrete of the traffic islands.

I'd like to think that the sight of these "invasives," feral and upstart, would have gladdened Concord's best-remembered son. There is in this Thoreauvian perspective on *natura naturans*. a hint of the Virgilian: a desire that seeks an order, a harmony, a peaceable kingdom. "We are wont to forget that the sun looks on our cultivated fields and on the prairies and forests without distinction," he wrote in *Walden*, pondering the fate of his famous beans. "In his view the earth is all equally cultivated like a garden. . . . This broad field which I have looked at so long looks not to me as the principal cultivator, but away from me to influences more genial to it, which water and make it green. These beans have results which are not harvested by me. Do they not grow for woodchucks partly? . . . Shall I not rejoice also at the profusion of the weeds whose seeds are the granary of the birds?"[12] The beans are cultivated not by an individual, but a community of forces and effects; their produce is a cornucopia open to all.

Thoreau would have appreciated the indomitability of *Ailanthus*; he would have seen it a renewal of the feral spirit that made the wild apples so appealing—and a promise that, drawing on its own treasury of excess, nature will ever find a way. For Thoreau, not unlike Spinoza before him, is looking at nature *naturing*—a process unfolding in and among creatures, forces, and landscapes that assemble themselves into things. Trees, when they come together, make a forest—an object recognizable across many striations of climate, biodiversity, and cultural entanglement: there are woodlands, timbers, taiga, the boreal, forests, jungles, copses, groves, thickets, and many other such assemblies, named and unnamed. But the effects and character of trees en masse, together in communities and assemblies, seem to comprise a notable and distinct class with ecological, cultural, and phenomenological dimensions. We have, in the tree as object, a forest of qualities and combinations.

Is the forest a system, a superorganism, an entity unto itself? To philosopher Alfred North Whitehead (1925), it was system that mattered. In *Science and the Modern World*, he compares the biographical quiddity of the individual tree to the life of the forest as a whole, and finds them strikingly out of sync. "A single tree by itself," Whitehead writes, "is dependent upon all the adverse chances of shifting circumstances. The wind stunts it: the variations in temperature check its foliage: the rains denude its soil: its leaves are blown away and are lost for the purpose of fertilisation." But such arbitrary accidents do not for Whitehead characterize the forces that fashion a forest, which form is the "normal way in which trees flourish." In the forest, "Each tree may lose something of its individual perfection of growth," Whitehead observes, "but they mutually assist each other in preserving the conditions for survival. The soil is preserved and shaded; and the microbes necessary for its fertility are neither scorched, nor frozen, nor washed away. A forest is the triumph of the organisation of mutually dependent species."[13]

To the environmental historian William Cronon however, those accidents of wind and rain are not mere epiphenomena, cancelling out in the forest's transcendent equilibrium. "Ecosystems have histories of their own," Cronon writes, which trump the "functionalist emphasis on equilibrium and climax" characteristic of classical ecology, with its models of orderly succession, and in which change is theorized as 'disturbance.'"[14] Cronon elaborates:

> Why a tree of a given species grew where it did was the result not only of ecological factors, such as climate, soil, and slope, but of history as well. A fire might shift a forest's composition from one group of species to another. A windstorm might blow over the mature trees of an entire tract of forest and allow the saplings growing beneath them to form a new canopy. Even a minor catastrophe, like the toppling of a single large tree, might create a microenvironment in the shadow of its uprooted base or in the sunlight of the newly broken canopy into which new species might move. . . . Events of this kind . . . constitute a history of the ecosystem in which a unique linear sequence was imposed on the regularly occurring processes which ecology as a science seeks to describe.[15]

How do we understand the forest for the trees? The science-studies scholar Chunglin Kwa identifies two ways of thinking about complexity, the *romantic* and the *baroque*, focusing respectively on the shapes systems take as wholes and the small, infinitely variable pieces that comprise them.[16] This latter, baroque model Kwa traces back to

Leibniz, who describes the natural world as a congeries of individual "monads" assembling themselves, with endless variety, into forms that are always arising and falling into decline. For Leibniz, it's monads all the way down, and in section 67 of the *Monadology* he evocatively describes the situation as follows: "Each portion of matter may be conceived as like a garden full of plants and like a pond full of fishes. But each branch of every plant, each member of every animal, each drop of its liquid parts, is also some such garden or pond."[17] For Leibniz, the trick is to see the forest *in* the tree.

The feral, I want to say, could be seen as a realization of the baroque; for feral things act as monads, each one of them reflecting a world in itself, and yet they're happy to act in assemblages that are always provisional confederations rather than cybernetic systems. In contrast we might say that the wild, under the sign of Darwinian evolution, is romantic in nature (Kwa considers Darwin a romantic). Evolution and ecology situate wildness in system, in which apex predator and tangled bank are parts of healthy, well-tempered ecosystems that, when in equilibrium, resist the shocks of individual events like fire and flood. Remember, however, that for the readers of Virgil in the time of the Roman republic, the predator, the fire, and the flood were demonic visitors from *beyond* the realm of nature. There are many ways to configure assemblages and individuals, systems and monads, forests and trees. And clearly, they are not equal: the Arboretum is a kind of forest, albeit one curated, designed, disciplined with great scientific and aesthetic specificity. And the monoculture of a tree farm is much different from a mature old-growth woodland, which is at once baroque in its bewildering variety and romantic in the dark glamor of its overwhelming, shadowy presence.

The charter of the forests

Of one thing I am certain: that with the romantic and the baroque, the wild and the feral, we have not begun to exhaust the forest. Indeed "forest" is an old word, though by no means the oldest associated with trees. Its origins stem from a distinction between wild timber and woodlands enclosed in parks; it takes its root from the Latin *foris* for "out doors." In England historically, forested lands were distinguished by their legal, and not their ecological, status. In *Forests of England*, John Croumbie Brown observes that a forest "must contain animals for the chase; trees or underwood for the shelter of them; and it must belong to the sovereign."[1] Thus a forest was not merely a stretch of woodland, but a resource enclosed in specific economic relations and a special connection to the monarchy. Such forests as Dean, Epping, and New Forest were part of a system of monarchical land holdings that helped to interrelate, coordinate, and control forms of vassalage, royal ritual, and subsistence. The medieval "forest," then, encompassed a legal domain with secondary attention to the trees it might enclose. "In regard to forests, we have it stated that, while a forest cannot be held by any but a Sovereign, a grant of one may, by a prescribed procedure, be made to a subject; but it, by this act, ceases to be a forest, and it is then designated a Chase, and it is not required that it be kept surrounded by an enclosure." There were further divisions and definitions: enclosed with fencing, a forest or chase becomes a park; a warren was a stretch of open land given over as preserve for small, cover-dependent game such as hares or partridges. Finally, there was the possibility of being a wood—a stretch of land covered in standing trees or copsewood—which could exist in a forest or outside of one (and a forest, in its medieval legal sense, might not contain any woods at all).

A woodland, in ceasing to be a forest in this medieval sense of the word, was said to be "disafforested," and "disafforestation" was to remove a stretch of woodland and its resources from the sole distributive powers of the monarch; thus, the state of being a "forest" was largely legal and not ecological. Although the state did have ecological consequences, akin to those of Cronon's wind-toppled tree; a disafforested woodland became open to the transformations of foraging in ways a royal forest was not.

The political economics of forests were at the heart of the controversy that led up to the writing of the Magna Carta—which was followed by a less well known, but more comprehensive charter of economic enfranchisement called the Charter of the Forests. Issued in 1215, the Magna Carta was drawn up as an agreement between King John and a group of rebel barons (often described as disgruntled); their concerns included the restive freemen under their vassalage, whose access to natural resources—their ability not only to hunt game and cut wood, but gather nuts, forage for crops, and make use of water for drinking, fish ponds, and power— had been implacably rolled back and curtailed by the Crown's "afforestation" and assertion of control over open lands.

The relations binding commoners and nobility through forests were ancient by the time of the Magna Carta, and deeply woven into the symbolism of Christian Europe. In 1215, the Fifth Crusade got under way, inspired by Philip of Oxford, who used the figure of the taming of the forest to allegorize the Christian mission: "In the beautiful wood of paradise death was hidden under the mantle of life, so, on the contrary, in the deformed and horrible wood life was hidden under the mantle of death, just as life is concealed, in the case of crusaders, under the mantle of a labor, which is like death."[2] By the thirteenth century, the forests had their own system of laws and networks of courts and officials; though often wild in appearance, they were precisely managed, their resources quantified down to the last acreage of pond or head of venison. When King John met the rebel barons at Runnymede, he answered their demands to recognize their own powers and liberties—but broader, popular concerns about the king's forests and the laws pertaining to them went unanswered. The people thus remained restive, and in 1217 a second document was drawn up and agreed, called the Charter of Forests.

Use of forestlands in medieval England had its own rich vocabulary: there was *agistment*, the practice of seasonally pasturing flocks and herds in forestlands to make use of the "common of herbage"; *pannage*, in which pigs were set loose in the forest to forage for acorns and beechnuts; and *estovers*, by which was meant the gathering of wood. Following J. M. Neeson, Peter Linebaugh evocatively catalogs the cornucopia of the medieval woodland:

Lops and tops or snap wood for the household, furze and weeds for fodder, bavins or sprays such as bakers and potters wanted for the ovens and kilns. [Neeson] notes where bean stakes could be found, how hazel was good for sheepfolds, how to assemble a chimney-sweeping brush. The woodlands were a reservoir of fuel; they were a larder of delicacies, a medicine chest of simples and cures. As for food, hazelnuts and chestnuts could be sold at market; autumn mushrooms flavored soups and stews. Wild chervil, fennel, mint, wild thyme, marjoram, borage, wild basil, tansy made herbs for cooking and healing. Wild sorrel, chicory, dandelion leaves, salad burnet, cats-ear, goats-beard, greater prickly lettuce, corn sow-thistle, fat-hen and chickweed, yarrow, charlock, and goose grass made salads. Elderberries, blackberries, bilberries, barberries, raspberries, wild strawberries, rosehips and haws, cranberries and sloes were good for jellies, jams, and wines.[3]

In the era of the Magna Carta, the church had threatened the nobility with excommunication for denying commoners access to woodland and field. Chapter 7 of the Magna Carta decreed that the widow "shall have . . . her reasonable estovers of commons."[4] The Charter of Forests recognized these practices not only as folkways and means of subsistence, but as *rights*, as fully recognized as the right to trial by jury, due process, habeas corpus, and freedom from cruel and unusual punishment, all enshrined in the Magna Carta. What the

Magna Carta and Charter of the Forests vouchsafed to commoners for some time—access to traditional, woodland resources for market and subsistence—was taken back by the nobility in the centuries that followed.

A crucial step in this long assault on the commons was the dissolution of the monasteries in 1536, when King Henry VIII, in a dispute with the Roman Catholic Church that was equal parts marital and political, seized the monasteries and their estates—some of the last repositories of common, accessible field and wood by the sixteenth century—and turned it over to favored private hands and selling it to finance his military expeditions. Thus began "a massive act of state-sponsored privatization," Linebaugh writes, which, "more than any other single act in the long history of the establishment of English private property ... made the English land a commodity."[5] These new landowners began to convert their property into cash by the quickest and most efficient means then available: throwing the common laborers off the land, clearing it, putting up fences and hedges, and pasturing sheep. The official translation of the charter prepared by one of Henry VIII's ministers omitted provisions acknowledging subsistence rights, making the Crown's ambitions jibe with a rewritten history.

Large trees were gone from English forests by the time colonists began their migration to North America in the seventeenth century. Those colonists were boggled by the profusion of wood in American forestlands—both the teeming multitudes of trees and the size they attained.

As the Royal Navy grew in the time following the defeat of the Spanish Armada, England's appetite for large logs became insatiable. The largest vessels carried mainmasts forty inches in diameter at the base—and a mast that size, according to a rule of thumb that gave a yard of length to every inch of thickness, would have topped out at 120 feet tall.[6] The English fought a series of naval wars with the Dutch in the seventeenth century to secure the strait connecting the North Sea with the Baltic, where the tallest and largest trees of Europe grew. Even these were too small, however, forcing the English to rely on "made masts" built of pieced-together lumber.

The trees of Maine's forests dwarfed those of the Baltic; some, reaching six feet or more in diameter and 200 feet in height, were too large to be carried by conventional ships. Early in the colonial history of North America, the Crown sought to reassert its ancient rights over forestland, levying a £100 fine for the cutting of such trees without royal license.[7] But Maine's Androscoggin and Piscataqua Rivers were beyond the practical reach even of the royal governor in Boston, and this regulation was largely ignored in the rush to denude New England of timber for fuel, housing, and industry. Colonists were profligate: the half-timber construction and thatch roofs common in early-modern England, practices which arose to answer the scarcity of lumber in Britain, were quickly abandoned by English settlers who preferred wooden shingles and clapboard siding, hallmarks of the "colonial" style in houses to this day.

Well into the twentieth century, the condition of American forests at the time of the colonies' establishment was understood as one of Edenic, unsullied abundance. "Three hundred years," historian William Carlton wrote in 1939, "*when human hands were not there with tools to cut them*, American forests grew until the decay of old age brought them down."[8] Now, Carlton's statement is troubling in its blindness to the seventeenth-century indigenous population of North America, but his presumption is a common one: that colonists came upon a waste and wilderness untouched by human hands, ripe for the taking. Into the second half of the twentieth century, Robert Frost could describe colonial North America as a "land vaguely realizing westward,/But still unstoried, artless, unenhanced," in his poem "The Gift Outright" (which, though it first appeared in 1942, was still considered fresh and relevant enough for Frost to recite at the inauguration of John F. Kennedy in 1961). The truth of American lands and forests was more complex. In southern New England especially, forestlands were a park-like mosaic of woodland and open savanna, created by indigenous North Americans through a careful program of burning. "Colonial observers understood burning as being part of Indian efforts to simplify hunting and facilitate travel," writes William Cronon, but "most failed to see its subtler ecological effects";[9] fire sped recycling of nutrients into the soil, encouraged the flourishing of berries and herbs, and discouraged swampy lowland trees in favor of oaks—all aspects of an indigenous program of forestry which, however subtle, was thorough in its effects.

By the nineteenth century, two hundred years of European-derived agriculture had transformed the indigenous mosaic of forage and low-intensity agriculture in a pastoral patchwork of cultivation, grazing, and production. In comparison to colonial descriptions of the seventeenth century's abundance, the woods and fields where Thoreau encountered his wild apples seemed "maimed" and "imperfect" to him. But Cronon asks, "What are we to make of the wholeness and perfection which he thought preceded it?"[10]

PART THREE

A DARK ABUNDANCE

The tree and/in history

As Thoreau predicted, the wild apple trees are gone from the woods and fields around Concord. In company with early New England farmers' livestock, and companionable wild animals, the trees made special forms, rhyming forms, responsive to shifting human and animal ways—to *history* in the expansive spirit William Cronon evokes. And as history, the shapes made by Thoreau's feral apple trees are likely gone forever, evoked only in words and traces, their roots confounded in the earth.

Someday, the feral ways of the Tree of Heaven will be gone as well—for if New York is one day covered with a forest of *Ailanthus*, the tree will have founded its own empire, and begun a new career, and its furtive, feral ways in the modern city will be set aside. These instances of senescence, of decline, are not precisely synonymous with *extinction* in biology's terms, nor of the rise and fall of forest biomes in succession, as described by classical ecology. These are the ways of trees, as they are of all objects in a dappled world, not trapped by a system of laws but swarming to assemble, to make friends and allies, and to swerve.

Of course trees differ from us in many ways, but one of the chief ones is almost purely geometric: while humans and most complex animals orient to the horizon, trees have organized their lives vertically. The "front" of the tree in some profound sense is its efflorescing canopy, questing sunward. Its progress in this quest is branching, manifold, many-fingered; its action in this work of sunward, vertical life is neither wholly active nor passive.

The tree expresses itself in the middle voice: *the tree growing* is a statement describing both the searching, volitional inexorability of living cells dividing, tissues using photoreactive compounds and a shimmering pallette of minerals to map light and gravity, sending sugars coursing across gradients of solubility, synthesizing hormones to impel cell division and senescence. But growing also inflects what happens to the tree in the form of history-making, individuating phenomena: the peculiar habits of light and temperature on *this* particular hillside; the seasonal prevalence of lightning or flooding on *this* particular plain. The tree's growth is happening along a dimension, the vertical; and yet is unfolding and ramifying into branches contrapuntally, polyvocally, the way choral voices radiate and overlay—braiding, swerving, and individual, and yet fusing into a single world of expression. The tree is a fugue of becoming, growing, worlding—and the voices of the trees in a forest in the same way are not monadal but modal, well tempered, choral.

French anthropologist Philippe Descola argues that we need to drop the symmetry (invidious and never entirely equal) between nature and culture in order to devote ourselves adequately to the full diversity of meaning-making with and through our entanglements with objects:

The stabilization in frameworks of thought and action of our practical engagement with the world—what one might call "worlding"—is based primarily upon our capacity to detect qualities in existing things and to consequently infer the links (I want to say, some of them) that they are susceptible to maintain and the actions of which they are capable. It thus hardly makes sense to oppose, as modernist epistemology does, a single and true world, composed of all the objects and phenomena potentially knowable, to the multiple and relative worlds that each one of us creates through our daily subjective experience. . . . Neither Platonic prototypes ready to be captured more or less completely by our faculties, nor pure social constructions that would give meaning and form to a raw material, the objects of our environment, material and immaterial, amount to packets of qualities of which certain are detected, others are ignored.[1]

I want to say, with Descola, that this superfluity of undetected and ignored qualities is a key aspect of the very possibility of culture—a necessary, grounding basis for the negotiation of shared symbolic entanglements. We need this darkling immanence to provide amplitude for tinkering with meaning in a world of dappled objects.

The artist Rachel Sussman spent the last few years chasing the oldest living things wherever they may be found around the world. Many of them—though not all—are trees. Her photographs, collected in her book *The Oldest Living Things in the World*, offer provisional and moving testimony to the ways life finds to abide, to persist, with grit and grace. She began her journey with the sequoias, millennia-old creatures, which stand in their ancient glory within reach of a rental-car journey from the great cities of California. The sequoias and redwoods of the west coast of North America are perhaps the chief symbol of vegetal longevity, the objective correlative of the long lives of trees. This longevity, crucial to the ways we do and think trees, is a key curatorial value in the preservation of sequoia groves and the ecosystems that accompany them, and the wildness of such places belies the careful curatorial attention they have come to receive. In Kings Canyon National Park, the locations of long-lived trees are marked on a document called a "stem map" which, in Sussman's description, is "reminiscent of a celestial navigation chart; the trees earthbound constellations."[2]

Take a sequoia, not only its age but its uncanny form of life: painted onto a core of heartwood thousands of years in the making, its rippled sheath of pluripotent meristem is both ancient and newly born—in a very real sense, ageless. The form of the tree, its branching arborescence, fills a cathedral volume with gestures and improvisations on Goethe's *Urpflanze*; its needled canopy, vast organ of photosynthesis, is equal parts all-seeing eye and ever-opening mouth. The robe of meristem has been rent into a fine lacework of holes; rainwater trickles into these tears, and wells, collects in the heartwood, bores deeper, gathers force and gushes out in geysers and springs. As needles age, they slough off and fall, collecting on the upper faces of the great boughs that jut outward like yardarms to windward; over the decades, the centuries, they compress, break down, are composted through the action of microbes, arthropods, and annelid worms. In a matter of years, whole trees of other species—red cedar, Douglas fir—have grown to appreciable girth in bough-borne humus 150 feet from the proper forest floor. A fire courses through the stand; a century later new growth has taken the place of charred needle and coal-barked limb, and yet the scars remain, registered indelibly in the archive of the architecture of the tree. Great blades of carbonized wood reach twenty, thirty feet up the trunk—and yet they don't come close to reach even the lowermost limbs, which emerge perhaps eighty feet from the ground. There is much in the lumber of this memory palace that is recoverable, legible, registered durably—and much else that resides beyond our ken, in an otherness deeply strange, far removed even from the anthropically adjacent alterities of dogs and fishes.

The oldest coast redwoods date back a millennium or more, and sequoias persist even longer. But to the east, beyond the Sierras, in the rain shadow of their alpine heights, another species of tree ekes out even longer lives. Twisted and carbuncled, among the bristlecone pines of California's White Mountains are living organisms whose biographies stretch back to before the rise of written records in human history. And like clay, papyrus, and stone, wood keeps its records well. "The burning of books and libraries has perhaps fallen out of fashion," writes Ross Andersen in his account of bristlecone's precarious longevity. "But if you look closely, you will find its spirit survives in another distinctly human activity, one as old as civilisation itself: the destruction of forests. Trees and forests are repositories of time; to destroy them is to destroy an irreplaceable record of the Earth's past."[3] To Andersen, the sere, splintered forests where bristlecone abides are "as dense with history as Alexandria." I'm grateful for Andersen's characterization of bristlecone time as "history," which calls to mind William Cronon's evocation of history in the occasion of a fallen-over tree in a New England forest, a minor but meaning-making revolution nestled in epochs of ecological unfolding: in the shelter of the upturned root-dome, a seedling takes root and sends leaves toward a new gap in the canopy; in a few years, new trees, new insects, fungi, birds; a new sense of arborescent order, of branching shade and dappled possibility. Even with no one there to hear it, the fallen tree resonates in time and place.

The history that bristlecone archives, however, does not belong to the species alone. Their growth rings treasure a climate archive stretching back millennia. Many trees offer such records, of course, and the study of dendrochronology, reading the climatological past in tree rings, is a well-established practice. Libraries of core samples taken from trees living and dead around the world establish a line of reference for the past stretching back some 11,000 years. In the bristlecones, climate scientists have one of the longest-established and continuous lines of reference, and one of the most legible, as the growth rings of trees in arid places respond more expressively to fluctuating conditions than trees in moist conditions, where the fatness of the land tends to run the rings together.

The bristlecones seek the arid cold found at altitude, and most of them are now found between nine and ten thousand feet, nestled in the chipped and broken dolomite slopes north of Death Valley. By seeking out such severe conditions, the bristlecones have found the secret of longevity, not a fountain but a high desert of youth; for relatively fewer boring insects brave the dry, thin air, and few other tree species seek out these vistas to steal sunlight from bristlecone's meager store of needles. Bristlecones divide their growing areas into sectors, radial pie-slices of trunk. Each sector of the bark makes its own independent channel from root to foliage-producing branch; damaged roots or broken limbs may kill a sector, but others will survive. Over the long life of a bristlecone, it can lose most of its sectors and still thrive as a thread or two of continuous growth. And survive they do: the oldest known bristlecone, the so-called Methuselah tree, is thought to be 4,800 years old. Each tree is thus a kind of forest or grove unto itself, a huddle of twisty sectional trees sharing a treasury of heartwood, bound together around a sheave of splinter and bole.

With and without us

It is late fall, all gleam and cold, and I've gone gleaning. In the Arboretum again, two shakes of the running shoes take me there, into the long pondside field where they plant the *Rosaceae*, which Wikipedia calls a "medium-sized family" of flowering plants—but which seems vast enough to me, encompassing not only the roses, but "apples, pears, quinces, apricots, plums, cherries, peaches, raspberries, loquats, and strawberries; almonds . . . meadowsweets, photinias, firethorns, rowans, and hawthorns." The flush of chill has reawakened my curiosity for quinces, as well as another rosaceous fruit, the medlar. Quinces and medlars, unlike their more marketable cousins, the apple and the pear, want to mellow on the branch long after they ripen; this softening into decay breaks down the astringent tannins, increases the sugars, and renders flesh that is darkened and grotty, spiced and rich. The process is known as bletting—a word that seems evocative and medieval to me, though it was only coined in the mid-nineteenth century.

In the field of roses, then, I slow my running to a stalk, and pace the long curving beds that are moistening toward winter. There's a long range of Dawson's crabapple, slender upswept branches hung with myriad fig-sized fruit that has rotted into tiny dimpled sacks. I pluck one and squeeze it into my palm; a clear liquid jets forth, which tastes of bright vinegar. Further on are cherries and crabapples of other kinds, fruit-fisted and small; a sorb tree sports berries of crimson dappled gold. I come to a bush like a sheaf of switches, whip-thin branches bound thickly together; strewn about on the mulch are droves of crumpled quinces bletted into mush. They are broken beyond redemption, however, and I'm unwilling to taste. Two of the fallen fruit seem newly ripe, however, still flaxen yellow and firm to the touch.

How we taste of trees, how we gather, how we glean. They arrive now in ranks and rows, in groves planted mechanically, sprayed and petted, traipsed in precariousness by migrant workers beating the boughs or climbing ladders to unsettle the fruit crop. We would do well to remember that in our political economy with the tree there is this originary intimacy, this reach to pluck and pull, to bite, to taste. There is always for us the gleam of a tree at the center of some garden, recalled, reimagined, promising—what?—some posture beyond ferality, some self-possessing domestication that transcends grafting knife and limb saws, that transcends discipline.

In the groves, in the vineyards, however, the fruiting trees demand our attention, call forth our labor. The *Georgics*, in which Virgil hymns the ways of Roman agriculture, is the Roman poet's documentary on the tilling and sowing of fields, the pasturage of flocks, the care of honeybees, and—not last, but taking priority in my account—the cultivation and care of trees, vines, and shrubs. His concern is the cultivation of trees for fruit and nut, and he celebrates the forceful creations of the nurseryman, whose craft makes strange and fruitful hybrids:

> in knotless trunks is hewn
> A breach, and deep into the solid grain
> A path with wedges cloven; then fruitful slips
> Are set herein, and—no long time—behold!
> To heaven upshot with teeming boughs, the tree
> Strange leaves admires and fruitage not its own.[1]

The poet is describing the horticultural practice of grafting, which can be used to repair damage, combine fruit-heavy boughs with hearty roots, or even to create arresting and unusual latticeworks of branches for furniture making. Typically, grafting is done using plants that are related, and Virgil's combinations are surprising: the arbutus (or madrone) with walnut; apple boughs installed on the limbs of the plane tree. Improbable pairings.

More credibly, Virgil describes the Roman vintner's practice of training grape vines to grow on trees, including that of the chestnut, whose strength and deep-rootedness contrast implicitly with wine's transient pleasures:

> The tree that props it, aesculus in chief,
> Which how so far its summit soars toward heaven,
> So deep strikes root into the vaults of hell.
> It therefore neither storms, nor blasts, nor showers
> Wrench from its bed; unshaken it abides,

Sees many a generation, many an age
Of men roll onward, and survives them all,
Stretching its titan arms and branches far,
Sole central pillar of a world of shade.[2]

And yet these cultivated vines, however deep-pillared by
the tree to which they're trained, fall prey readily to the
depredations of fire:

> . . . for oft from careless swains
> A spark hath fallen, that,' neath the unctuous rind
> Hid thief-like first, now grips the tough tree-bole,
> And mounting to the leaves on high, sends forth
> A roar to heaven, then coursing through the boughs
> And airy summits reigns victoriously,
> Wraps all the grove in robes of fire, and gross
> With pitch-black vapour heaves the murky reek
> Skyward, but chiefly if a storm has swooped
> Down on the forest, and a driving wind
> Rolls up the conflagration. When'tis so,
> Their root-force fails them, nor, when lopped away,
> Can they recover, and from the earth beneath
> Spring to like verdure; thus alone survives
> The bare wild olive with its bitter leaves.[3]

It's notable that Virgil claims that it's the *wild* olive tree that
is hardy enough to withstand fire, distinct in that respect
from its cosseted, cultivated, domestic kin. For Romans in

the era of the republic, the classicist David O. Ross points out, "nature" was that which man tilled and cultivated. Ross describes the Roman understanding of nature as nearly the opposite of our own, rooted in the cycles of agriculture, with cultivation the deepest expression and even generation of nature itself. The forces of the storm, of wind and volcano and wild animal: these were divine energies visited from *beyond* upon the natural realm—man and his fields, his beasts, his orchards. Ross finds the basis for this argument in the etymology of *natura* itself, which emerges as a word for birth and things born into the world. To the Romans, says Ross,

> "Nature" is agricultural, is inconceivable without man, and is his creation: but herein lies, and lay, an obvious paradox, which is indeed a central paradox for the Georgics. . . . For the Romans, I think, the storm that destroys and the pests that attack are un-natural, are forces dire and hostile . . . whereas the grain and vine are the embodiment of the natural cycles of life.[4]

Much has intruded into our understanding of *natura* since Virgil's time. In addition to hymning the stateliness and sturdiness of my front-yard oak with its titan arms and teeming boughs, for example, a latter-day Virgil could sing of qualities more modern in flavor: name it as an angiosperm and member of the dicotyledonae, an erstwhile and deprecated taxon; counted in the order Fagales, which also includes the beeches, walnuts, birches, and bayberries; describe it as a biochemical reactor producing such phenolic compounds as Grandinin/roburin E, castalagin/vescalagin, gallic acid, monogalloyl glucose (glucogallin) and valoneic acid dilactone, monogalloyl glucose, digalloyl glucose, trigalloyl glucose, quercitrin and ellagic acid—toxic and aromatic substances that arise in response to disease, pathogen, and injury; could note that its wood, calculable in board feet, is a vast treasury of xylem, a slow-flowing collision of cellulose fibers enjambed within a matrix of lignin and shot through with tyloses, microscopic outgrowths that collapse into the vessels of disused xylem to lend structure and great strength to the wood; could chant the explosion of animal vigor within this house of many mansions, sheltering life forms from the protozoan to the passerine; call it *Quercus alba* in the binomial system of Linnaeus, who described it on the basis of leaves brought from North America, noting also that it's white oak to the wise and the big tree on the corner to the neighbor kids; and sing on of who-knows-what archipelago of sweet, secret appellations among its dark menagerie. *All that which moves outside our sort of why*, indeed.

Like Virgil, we treat trees as objects in daily life; like Auden's object, they seem content to keep to their own edges. Or do they? There is an old, squat maple tree in a cemetery near my house, which some years ago was struck by a backhoe or some other machine; the heartwood rotted in the scar, turning to humus, which induced the living vascular tissue above the injury to send roots into the heart of the tree itself.

Even within itself, a tree will not to its own edges keep. And the forms trees take in connection with human lifeworlds, meanwhile, engage the full panoply of our entanglement with questions of materiality, community, and design. As objects, trees inhabit or create an uncanny space in which they seem sessile, passive, pliably responsive to human acts and needs; and yet they carry on abundant and active lives of their own, with qualities and even varieties of affect remote to our experience. In their endlessly varying ways of taking up residence in proximity to the human, trees refract the dappled light of myriad material and biologic possibilities into a vast array of quotidian human experiences. Their forms suggest ways of organizing data, institutions, and knowledge (and even knowledge about trees themselves may be found subsumed in tree-like diagrams). And with the great ages they are capable of reaching, they express something ineffable and awe-inspiring about the vigor and capacities of life on earth. The longevity, endurance, and stock-still stability of even the most familiar street trees is awesome, an instance of the sublime: for we come to trees—the old ones, anyway, which surround us, enfold us, embower us—as beginners, as newcomers to arborescent forms of life well under way.

Bound within their rings in circle upon circle reaching back to sapling seasons, trees treasure up the carbon they capture from the atmosphere, metabolizing CO_2 through photosynthesis to make sugars and build wood. Tree-like plants have been doing this work for nearly four hundred million years; the thick black vein of coal encircling the planet dates from the rise of the tree as a dominant form of life on the planet. This sequestration of carbon transformed global climate long before the rise of humans, or even mammals, but we've only begun to pay attention to it in the last few decades. Archive, waste repository, storyteller and world-maker—add these to the ways we've learned to do and think the tree.

We've flooded our atmosphere with carbon, an element which is little more than trees *in potentia*, in airy solution, as-yet evanescent and imaginal, waiting to arrive. And waiting is what the trees do. Breeze-blown, deciduous or evergreen, heavy with fruit or with leaves senescent flying, the trees abide. Thoreau imagined a human world of pasture and fieldstone fence without feral apple trees; now, we're forced to contemplate a world of trees without us. In our most desperate watches, we wonder how long it will take the trees to sequester our spent carbon credits, to pull the vagrant CO_2 down into their boughs, leaves, and roots, to treasure it up again in the layers of the earth. To do this work—to slowly unfold through millennia of slow-receding warmth the full measure of their dark abundance—without us.

As an object, a life form, and a form of life, the tree was already ancient when humankind came into the world. And yet we have walked many an age in tandem with trees, following and followed in turn, from continent to continent around the globe. Trees have made human forms of life possible—and those human lifeways have opened new ways for trees in the world as well. The whole career of written history has passed during the time it has taken for a few individual trees to grow from sapling to maturity—so much human activity passing like a shadow, a mid-day blur, evanescent in the sequoia's dappled precincts. For such a tree, the days are minutiae— moments, which pass too fast for registration. Seasons are the days of tree-time, of lives measured out on the scale of glaciers and climatic epochs. This longer, slower view of time is one we might want to adopt; for in our own way, we've lately discovered, we humans have taken on the capacity to act with epoch-making force on the planet's climate. Even now, the bristlecones, like many alpine and high-country plant species, strive to climb higher and higher to escape the warming temperatures of climate change. We call this change anthropogenic, and the age that it will likely characterize, the Anthropocene. And yet I don't think we should be so quick to attribute these effects to any fundamental nature we have as a species. Climate change is the result of specific social and economic relations in human history: how we in the West, in a lineage reaching back to Virgil with his divine powers arriving from outside of Nature, have come to perceive the value of resources, landscapes, and living things. We might do better, I think, to call this age the *Occidentocene*, in light of the Western ways that set it in motion.

Can a tree be feral? I return to my starting question with the sense that, in this emergent Anthropocene, ferality indeed might offer the best hope for trees, and a boost for human prospects as well. I'm back with the copse of *Ailanthus* in Bussey Brook Meadow, watching their lithe boles bend springily in the city breeze. A steel howl rises from beyond the trees where the Acela train slices through the neighborhood on its way out of the city; lazy motes of passenger jets high above contrast with the staccato flocks of sparrows rippling the sky into tweed. On the tangled bank of the mesa, refuse peeks out from beneath the bittersweet underbrush: a bruised shoe, a tangle of copper flashing, a torn page of roofing paper, all nestle together in the loose black soil. And the slender *Ailanthus*, towering above, dapple these mingled objects and the promiscuous vines with a softening light. Throughout the city, stands of *Ailanthus* such as this mark provisional and temporary demarcations of property; they fill the vacant lots, springing from amid the tires and wreckage of fences. They shelter the trash-pickers and the gleaners, clutch and hold the poisoned soils that would otherwise run off the salvage lots into sewers that flow into Boston Harbor. These trees treasure up their carbon in dark abundance, in compounds that compose fungible resources of elemental matter and overflowing possibility. A century ago, from the dizzy imperial heights of industrial progress, it was possible to envision the city after us returning to wild forest; today, we might do better to acknowledge that a city is a feral forest, always and already; to know that forms of life are forever branching, and that bewilderment is our natural habitat.

NOTES

The tree of heaven

1 Peter Del Tredici, *Wild Urban Plants of the Northeast* (Cornell: Cornell University Press, 2010).

2 Nancy Chen, "'Speaking Nearby': A Conversation with Trinh T. Minh-ha," *Visual Anthropology* 8, no. 1 (1992): 81–92.

3 Betty Smith, *A Tree Grows in Brooklyn* (New York: Harper Bros., 1943), 6.

4 F. W. Bailey, "Ailanthus," in *The American Botanist, Devoted to Economic and Ecological Botany*, vols. 11–15, ed. Willard Nelson Clute (Joliet: Clute & Co., 1911), 37.

In a dappled world

1 Nancy Cartwright, *The Dappled World: A Study of the Boundaries of Science* (Cambridge: Cambridge University Press, 1992), 1.

2 Aldo Leopold, *A Sand County Almanac: With Other Essays on Conservation from Round River* (Oxford: Oxford University Press, 1949), 225.

3   Edward James Salisbury, *Weeds and Aliens* (London: Collins, 1964).

4   Peter Del Tredici, *Wild Urban Plants of the Northeast*, back cover text.

5   Salisbury, *Weeds and Aliens*, 23.

6   Ibid.

7   Ibid., 86.

8   Donna Haraway, *The Companion Species Manifesto: Dogs, People, and Significant Otherness* (Chicago: Prickly Paradigm, 2003), 5.

9   Leopold, *Sand County*, 204.

A branching heuristic

1   In what follows I'm using the Greimas Square, a kind of heuristic schema used in semiotics; my favorite example of its use is in Rosalind Krauss, "Sculpture in the Expanded Field," *October* 8 (Spring, 1979): 30–44.

2   Sigmund Freud, *The Uncanny*, translated by David McLintock (New York: Penguin, 2003).

3   Mary Douglas, *Purity and Danger: An Analysis of Concepts of Pollution and Taboo*, Collected Works, Volume II (London and New York: Routledge, 2003), 36.

4   George W. S. Trow, *Within the Context of No Context* (New York: Atlantic Monthly Press, 1997). The feral quality of having no qualities was most famously charted by Robert Musil in his novel *The Man Without Qualities*.

5   William James, *A Pluralistic Universe: Hibbert Lectures at Manchester College on the Present State of Philosophy* (New York: Longmans, 1909), 286.

6 For a polemical take on "rewilding," see George S. Monbiot's *Feral: Rewilding the Land, the Sea, and Human Life* (Chicago: University of Chicago Press, 2015)—although Monbiot's concept of the "feral" is different from mine.

7 Samuel Johnson, *A Dictionary of the English Language* (London: 1785). Retrieved August 15, 2015 from https://archive.org/stream/dictionaryofengl01johnuoft#page/n251/mode/2up

In the tree museum

1 Iasmine A. B. S. Alves, Henrique M. Miranda, Luiz A. L. Soares, and Karina P. Randau, "Simaroubaceae Family: Botany, Chemical Composition and Biological Activities," *Revista Brasileira de Farmacognosia* 24, no. 4 (2014): 481–501. Retrieved August 15, 2015, from http://www.scielo.br/scielo.php?script=sci_arttext&pid=S0102-695X2014000400481&lng=en&tlng=en. 10.1016/j.bjp.2014.07.021

2 Alfred Rehder, *Bibliography of Cultivated Trees and Shrubs Hardy in the Cooler Temperate Regions of the Northern Hemisphere* (Jamaica Plain: Arnold Arboretum of Harvard University, 1949).

3 Yanni Loukissas, "The Life and Death of Data" (2014), http://lifeanddeathofdata.org.

4 See Ida Hay, *Science in the Pleasure Ground: A History of the Arnold Arboretum* (Boston: Northeastern, 1994).

5 Frederick Law Olmsted, "Public Parks and the Enlargement of Towns," in *Writing About Architecture: Mastering the Language of Buildings and Cities*, ed. Alexandra Lange (New York: Princeton Architectural Press, 2012), 123.

6 Hay, *Science*, 3.

7 W. H. Auden, "Objects," *Encounter* (January 1957): 67.

8 William Friedman (Director of the Arnold Arboretum), Facebook post, August 15, 2015, https://www.facebook.com/william.friedman.583

9 Loukissas, "Life and Death."

10 Agreement (Draft) Between the City of Boston Conservation Commission and the Arnold Arboretum of Harvard University. Operations and Maintenance Plan for the Bussey Brook Meadow Revised May 3, 2012. Arnold Arboretum, document shared with the author.

From *Ailanthus* to apple

1 Henry David Thoreau, "Wild Apples," *The Atlantic Monthly* 10, no. 5 (November 1862): 513–26. Digital version, http://www.theatlantic.com/past/docs/issues/1862nov/186211thoreau.htm (accessed August 15, 2015).

2 Thoreau, "Wild Apples."

3 Ibid.

4 Ibid.

5 Peter Del Tredici, "Gestalt Dendrology: Looking at the Whole Tree," *Arnoldia* 61, no. 4 (2002): 3.

6 Johann Wolfgang von Goethe, "Preliminary Notes for a Physiology of Plants," 1790.

7 Tristan Gooley, *The Natural Navigator* (London: Virgin Books, 2010).

8 Thoreau, "Wild Apples."

9 Ibid.

10 See, in the Emerson Papers in Houghton Library, Trees [1836–74]. A.MS.s.; Concord, 1836–74. 54f. (108p.)

11 Ralph Waldo Emerson, "Eulogy for Thoreau," *The Atlantic Monthly* (May 1862).

12 Henry David Thoreau, *Walden, and On the Duty of Civil Disobedience*, Project Gutenberg edition produced by Judith Boss and David Widger, 1995, http://www.gutenberg.org/files/205/205-h/205-h.htm (accessed July 25, 2015).

13 Alfred North Whitehead, *Science and the Modern World* (New York: Pelican, 1948).

14 William Cronon, *Changes in the Land: Indians, Colonists, and the Ecology of New England* (New York: Hill & Wang, 1983), 10–11.

15 Cronon, *Changes*, 32–33.

16 Chunglin Kwa, "Romantic and Baroque in the Sciences of the Complex," in *Complexities: Social Studies of Knowledge Practices*, ed. John Law and Annemarie Mol (Durham: Duke University Press, 2002), 23–52.

17 W. G. Leibniz, *The Monadology and Other Philosophical Writings*, translated by Robert Latta (London: Oxford University Press, 1898), 256.

The charter of the forests

1 John Croumbie Brown, *Forests of England in Bye-Gone Times* (Edinburgh: Oliver and Boyd, 1883), 17.

2 Peter Linebaugh, *The Magna Carta Manifesto* (Berkeley: University of California, 2008), 27.

3 Linebaugh, *Magna Carta*, 43.

4 Ibid., 52.

5 Ibid., 42.

6 William R. Carlton, "New England Masts and the King's Navy," *New England Quarterly* 12, nos. 4–18 (1939): 4.

7 Cronon, *Changes*, 110.

8 Carlton, "New England," 4.

9 Cronon, *Changes*, 50–51.

10 Ibid., 12.

The tree and in history

1 Phillippe Descola, *The Ecology of Others*, translated by Geneviève Godbout and Benjamin P. Luley (Chicago: Prickly Paradigm, 2013), 78.

2 Rachel Sussman, *The Oldest Living Things in the World* (Chicago: University of Chicago Press, 2014), 9.

3 Ross Andersen, "The Vanishing Groves," *Aeon Magazine*, October 16, 2012, http://aeon.co/magazine/science/ross-andersen-bristlecone-pines-anthropocene/

With and without us

1 Virgil's *Georgics*, in J. B. Greenough, *Bucolics, Aeneid, and Georgics of Vergil* (Boston: Ginn & Co., 1898), 2.68–80.

2 Virgil's *Georgics*, 2.292–300.

3 Ibid., 2.305–19.

4 David O. Ross, *Virgil's Elements: Physics and Poetry in the Georgics* (Princeton: Princeton University Press, 1987).

INDEX

Page references for illustrations appear in *italics*.